PERSONALITY AND
EDUCATIONAL ACHIEVEMENT

Personality and Educational Achievement
is the second volume in the *Educational
Achievement* series, under the general
editorship of Eric Gaudry. The first volume
of the series is *Anxiety and Educational
Achievement*, by E. Gaudry and C. D.
Spielberger. Other volumes are planned in
the following areas: Intelligence and
Creativity; Technology; Cognitive Develop-
ment; Perceptual Processes; Teaching
Strategies; and Social/Psychological
Factors.

Personality and Educational Achievement

F. D. Naylor
University of Melbourne

John Wiley & Sons Australasia Pty Ltd
SYDNEY   New York   London   Toronto

ISBN and National Library of Australia Card Number:
  Cloth: 0 471 63074-8
  Paper: 0 471 63075-6
Library of Congress Catalog Card Number: 72-1570

Registered at the General Post Office, Sydney, for
transmission through the post as a book.

Printed at The Griffin Press, Adelaide, South Australia

Contents

Preface

The primary aim of this book is the gathering together of the voluminous and scattered research on the relation between personality and achievement in school. For psychologists the area of personality has been a focus of research and theory for many years; and its relation to achievement has been intensively studied, particularly during the last decade. Teachers have become increasingly interested in the area as the movement to individualise instruction has gathered strength. There is a growing awareness that learning conditions which provide optimal opportunity for one pupil may not suit another pupil with different personality traits.

The fact that individual differences in intelligence cannot account for all or even the major part of the differences in achievement, suggests that personality variables may play a significant role in determining performance in school. This book looks at the problem of discrepant achievement, and the relation of adjustment and other personality variables to performance. The review does not attempt to be exhaustive in its scope; it assesses the current status of the research findings within the limits which have been set.

The studies reviewed are taken from American, Australian and British settings. They have been chosen as examples of the application of personality theories to the problem of understanding achievement in the classroom. It is hoped that the reader's interest in the psychology of personality will be stimulated, and that he will consult more basic sources. The readings in the second part of the book provide first-hand accounts of relevant and original research.

The editorial work on this volume was carried out by Eric Gaudry. I am especially grateful to him for his critical appraisals and helpful suggestions concerning the form and content of the manuscript. My thanks are due to the following individuals and organisations who gave kind permission to reproduce tables, figures and the articles selected for reading: M. Ainsworth, H. J. Butcher, R. B. Cattell, F. N. Cox, S. Cunningham, N. J. Entwistle, A. V. Everett, H. J. Eysenck, W. W. Farquar, D. S. Finlayson, E. Gaudry, I. E. Gordon, L. Jacobson, R. Lynn, E. L. McCallon, A. H. Matlin, F. H. Mendelsohn, J. E. Nesbitt, J. A. Oakland, R. Rosenthal, J. Rushton, R. D. Savage, A. P. Sealey, A. B. Sweney, R. G. Taylor, *Australian Journal of Education,*

British Journal of Educational Psychology, Journal of Counseling Psychology, Journal of Educational Research, Journal of Experimental Education, Psychological Reports, Routledge and Kegan Paul.

Melbourne   F. D. NAYLOR
March, 1972

Part One

Chapter 1

Introduction

The aim of this book is to consider some of the evidence concerning the relation between personality variables and school attainment. The major emphasis will be on research findings in this area, rather than on the implications of theories or the opinions of eminent educationists. However, some reference will be made to theories which bear directly on the empirical research findings. As the book progresses it will become apparent that research in this area has been rather piecemeal and unintegrated. Nonetheless both psychologists and teachers believe that the personality characteristics of pupils are important in accounting for their performances in school, particularly when those performances depart from what would be expected on the basis of the pupils' abilities. On this account the nature of the research findings is important in informing the opinions we might hold.

What is Personality?

It is convenient to distinguish two sorts of personality variables. This distinction is relative rather than absolute, but it is not entirely arbitrary. The first sort of variable may be called *structural* or static. Variables of this sort are considered to be relatively permanent or enduring qualities of individuals. Under normal circumstances they are held to be resistant to change. Some of these variables, such as introversion-extraversion, are assumed to be constitutionally or genetically based (Eysenck[1]), and, if this is true, it makes sense to regard them as static or structural qualities of individuals. Similarly, Cattell's source traits of personality (Cattell[2]) are those qualities of the personality which are considered to be relatively enduring. Intelligence is thought to be a largely inherited structural quality (Burt[3]), and obviously a biological characteristic such as sex can be regarded as a structural quality. Of course there would be individual differences in the *degree* to which such qualities are possessed; but the *kinds* of qualities are assumed to be common to everyone.

The second sort of variable may be called *dynamic* in that it is subject to change, generally as a function of changes in other circumstances. Such variables are frequently regarded as motivational in character, which suggests that they possess an energising or directing function in behaviour. On the other hand they may also be complex emotional reactions to situations of stress. Spielberger[4] put forward a theory of anxiety which distinguished anxiety as a relatively stable personality trait (*A*-Trait) from anxiety as a transitory emotional state (*A*-State). These variables are related to each other and to educational achievement in a variety of ways (Gaudry and Spielberger[5]). They provide an excellent example of the distinction being made here, in that they serve different theoretical functions by accounting for different classes of behaviour.

We shall resist the temptation to stipulate how personality should be defined. There is no uniquely psychological definition. However, our concern in this book will be with the relation of achievement in school to some personality variables which can be regarded as relatively static or structural. Variables either purely or strictly motivational in character have been disregarded, as such considerations would take us too far afield; limits have been imposed in order to establish a basic theme in a complicated area of research.

Personality Variables as Constructs

The kinds of structural and functional variables which are thought to constitute personality differ considerably in the various theories (Hall and Lindzey;[6] Bischof;[7] Pervin[8]). Personality is an abstraction and therefore there is a tendency to conceptualise it in different ways according to the kinds of qualities which the theorist abstracts. Consequently there is no general agreement among psychologists on a definition of personality even though they often agree about many of the variables constituting it. Congruence of definitions and compatibility in the measurement of personality variables become very important if the results of different studies are to be compared. It cannot be assumed that two different personality inventories, such as the Maudsley Personality Inventory (Eysenck[9]) and the 16PF (Cattell and Eber[10]), necessarily measure the same variables merely because they are both referred to as personality inventories. As we shall see when we come to consider factor analytic studies of personality in some detail, it is not always clear or self-evident just which personality variables are being measured.

What is being measured is generally regarded as a *construct*, but constructs can have different kinds of logical status (MacCorquodale and Meehl;[11] O'Neil;[12] Maze;[13] Meissner;[14] McLaughlin and Precians;[15] Naylor[16]). Some constructs are *relations*, which means that they are not entities, states or processes (or anything which can exist in logical independence of anything else), but rather the relations between such things. Thus learning, as a construct, might be regarded as the *relation* between certain manipulations of a pupil's environment ("teaching") and certain changes in his performance (say, from low to high achievement.) In these circumstances the truth of statements concerning the pupil's learning is equivalent to the truth of statements concerning the relation between "teaching" and changes in achievement level.

Other constructs are regarded as *qualities*, which are hypothetical states, entities, processes and so on, whose qualitative presence is inferred from behaviour. Personality traits such as "conscientiousness" or "dependence" might, as constructs, be regarded as *qualities* which an individual possesses in some degree. The truth of statements concerning such qualities is not equivalent to the truth of any other statements, but it is necessary for us to assume or hypothesise their existence if we desire to *explain* relations, such as the one above. This means that if such a hypothesis is true, certain observable consequences will follow. However, it should be noted that even if such consequences do follow as matters of fact, this does *not* show or prove that the hypothesis is true. All we can say is that the hypothesis has not been shown to be false. If the observational consequences turned out to be other than predicted then the hypothesis would be falsified, and therefore would have to be rejected.

These considerations indicate that we must be careful not to be misled by confusions between relations and qualities on the one hand and between different qualities on the other. As we shall see in Chapter 3, although different investigators refer to adjustment as a quality which an individual possesses in some degree, it does not inevitably follow that they are referring to the same thing. In so far as there are real differences in the quality referred to, we should not be surprised if different studies yield different results. Such differences become clear not only in the way such qualities are defined, but also in the way the investigator attempts to measure them. When different studies yield contradictory results we should take care to establish that the investigators are in fact referring to similar constructs, and that they are measuring them in compatible ways.

As Kerlinger[17] points out, the fact that a particular measure discriminates between two groups does not signify that the discrimination is a valid one. The theoretical value of any personality construct depends on its capacity to enter into a wide range of predictions from theory. As we shall see in Chapter 6, predictions concerning academic achievement from measures of the construct introversion-extraversion yield different results at different levels of education (e.g. Savage[18, 19]). No theory of introversion-extraversion satisfactorily explains these differences, and hence these different relations are poorly understood.

The value of any particular personality measure depends on its construct validity (Cronbach[20]), that is, on the degree to which it is a true measure of the construct in question. Contradictory results could indicate that the measures have poor construct validity, and/or that the constructs on which they are based are either relational or possess no predictive power. In neither case would it be possible to further our understanding or assert that the observed relations had been explained.

The summary point to be made here is that the words which are used to designate constructs do not necessarily have similar meanings for different investigators. This fact highlights the importance of theories of personality in informing research. A consistent and coherent theory makes clear the qualitative definitions of its constructs and the relations which hold between them; so that an investigator using the theory as a point of departure for research is in no doubt about the propositions of that theory. Construct validity requires that the measures of the constructs be similarly unambiguous.

Personality Assessment

The scientific assessment of personality is important for two reasons. First, the development of personality' theory through the testing of hypotheses requires the existence of reliable and valid measures of personality variables. Second, the assessment of personality measures is involved in the application of psychological techniques to education, in areas such as guidance, counselling, selection, remedial diagnosis and so on. It is not possible here to review the whole field of personality assessment. Since our concern is with the research which bears on the relation between personality and educational attainment, the kinds of assessment techniques which have been used in the reported research will be briefly discussed. More detailed discussion of the techniques of assessment and the issues involved can be found in Vernon.[21]

SELF-REPORT MEASURES

Most of the measures used in the reported research are of the self-report variety, largely taking the form of questionnaires and inventories. The advantage of these techniques is that usually they are easily administered to large groups in a fairly short time. The objective scoring methods which are generally used minimise interpreter biases in assigning scores. Questionnaires and inventories such as the High School Personality Questionnaire (Cattell and Cattell[22]) and the Eysenck Personality Inventory (EPI) (Eysenck and Eysenck[23]) have been widely used in research on the relation between personality and achievement.

The major disadvantage of these techniques is their susceptibility to faking and distortion (Vernon[21]). Subjects responding to the items might lie about an item's applicability to them; or they might distort their responses owing to the operation of response sets stimulated by either the social desirability of an item or a tendency to agree with what an item proposes (Edwards[24]). Eysenck and Eysenck[23] have incorporated a lie scale into the EPI. When scores on this scale exceed a certain value, responses to the remaining items are automatically invalidated. The influences of social desirability are less readily dealt with. In the Edwards Personal Preference Schedule (Edwards[25]) a forced choice technique is adopted which requires the testee to choose one of a pair of statements which have been previously equated for social desirability. However, its influence in other kinds of inventories is difficult to determine.

PROJECTIVE TECHNIQUES

Clinical psychologists commonly employ these techniques in the assessment of personality. In the inventory and questionnaire approach to assessment, the elicitation of responses takes place in a highly controlled situation. The test instructions are generally standardised to ensure uniformity of presentation in different groups. By this means, one test result is comparable with any other. In projective techniques the test setting and instructions are generally more unstructured in order to encourage a more free-flowing style of responsiveness. The available responses are thereby not completely predetermined by the test, and the testee is held to be less aware of any implicit requirements on the part of the tester. However, projective techniques have been severely criticised (e.g. Zubin;[26] Eysenck[27]) for their lack of reliability and validity, and their sloppy theoretical base. Vernon[21] is more sympathetic to their possibilities, but he is fully aware of their shortcomings. He remarks that they have obvious value when used as exploratory instruments.

Some studies will be referred to in which projective techniques have been used to assess particular personality characteristics (Cox[28]).

SEMANTIC DIFFERENTIAL TECHNIQUES

A semantic differential (Osgood, Suci and Tannenbaum[29]) possesses some of the more indirect characteristics of projective techniques, while at the same time it can be objectively scored. It is a very flexible technique in that it can be formulated in terms of the requirements of a particular research problem (Nunnally[30]). Testees rate concepts on a set of bipolar adjectival scales. The concepts and scales are generally chosen in terms of the problem being researched. The ratings of different concepts can be compared for their degree of similarity-dissimilarity, and the degree to which different concepts have similar meanings for an individual is inferred from these comparisons.

More details of this technique will be given in Chapter 3 where its application in a particular research setting will be discussed.

The Prediction of School Achievement

The prediction of school achievement from the measured abilities of pupils has a history going back to the turn of the century. The last half-century has seen the widespread application of intelligence tests to the selection of pupils for particular educational experiences. The streaming of pupils in homogeneous ability groups meant that teachers did not have to cope with wide individual differences in ability among pupils, and thereby the educational goals required by a fixed curriculum were more easily and economically attained. The "Eleven-plus" examination in England has used both intelligence and attainment tests as a basis of selection for secondary school.

Abilities and achievement are positively related, which is to say that high ability tends to go with high achievement, and low ability with low achievement. However, it should be noted that this is a tendency, not a one-to-one relation. Variables other than abilities, which are separate from them both empirically and theoretically, are therefore also positively related to performance.

It is possible to express such relations in quantitative form, and all the research studies which will be discussed express their results quantitatively. Quantitative statements of the relations between variables can be made using the product moment correlation coefficient r. The value of *r* between two variables expresses the degree and kind of their relationship. The size of *r* may vary from $+1\cdot00$ through zero to $-1\cdot00$, and its magnitude indicates the degree of relation. Its sign—plus or minus—indicates the kind of relation: positive or negative. When $r = +1\cdot00$ there is a perfect positive relationship between two variables: thus, for any given value of one variable, the value of the other is completely determined such that increases in score on both variables go together. A graphical representation of $r = +1\cdot00$ is shown in Fig. 1.1. As you can see, for any value of *X* the value of *Y* is completely determined, and vice versa.

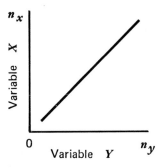

Fig. I.I Graphical representation of $r = +1\cdot00$.

Where $r = -1\cdot00$ there is a perfect negative relationship between two variables. Again, for any value of *X* the value of *Y* is completely determined, and vice versa. A graphical representation of $r = -1\cdot00$ is shown in Fig. 1.2.

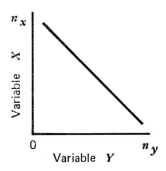

Fig. I.2 Graphical representation of $r = -1\cdot00$.

Here increases in score on one variable accompany decreases in score on the other.

Where $r = 0\cdot00$ there is no relationship between the variables, and hence it is not possible to predict a score on one from a score on the other. The graphical representation in Fig. 1.3 shows how tallies of the scores on the *X* and *Y* variable tend to cluster when $r = 0\cdot00$.

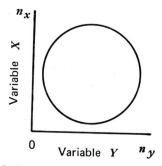

Fig. I.3 Graphical representation of $r = 0.00$.

Values of r between zero and plus or minus one occur frequently when variables are related. Perfect relations ($r = +1$ or -1) are rarely obtained in practice, either because of imperfect relations between variables in fact, or because of errors in our measurement of the variables. As the magnitude of r increases from zero to $+1.00$, so the degree of positive relation between the variables increases. In contrast, as the magnitude of r changes from zero to -1.00 so the degree of negative relation between the variables increases. Thus the higher the value of r the greater the degree of positive or negative relation, depending on the sign of the value of r. Fig. 1.4 shows how, for various values of r, the tallies of scores on the two variables X and Y would tend to cluster. The shapes of the ellipses indicate the shapes of the clusters.

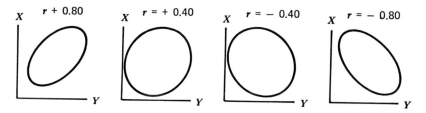

Fig. I.4 The cluster shapes of tallies of scores for four values of r.

Correlations often form the basis for the application of a mathematical technique called factor analysis which has been widely used in the study of personality and the construction of personality measures (e.g. Cattell[2]). It is used to reduce a matrix of correlation coefficients among many pairs of variables to a more basic set of variables called factors. Cattell's source traits and Eysenck's personality types are based on factor analysis. In Chapter 4 we shall consider some of the psychological aspects of factor analysis. This will form a basis for the discussion of the relations between personality traits and achievement in Chapters 5 and 6.

Intelligence and school achievement are known to be correlated (e.g. Butcher[31]). The value of r between these two variables itself varies; it is not a permanent, fixed quantity. It is subject to the influences of the motivational condition of the pupil, his personality characteristics, the characteristics of the teacher and the learning environment, what is being taught, and so on. However, as Cattell[2] points out, the typical value of the correlation between intelligence and attainment is around $r = +0.50$. A value of $r = +1.00$ has never been reported, so that even though occasionally the value might be greater than 0.50, it never reaches unity. This implies that some part of the individual differences in attainment can be accounted for by differences in intelligence. The question is: how much?

All the variables which combine together to determine school performance can be regarded as a finite universe of qualities totalling 100 per cent. This is referred to as the total *variance*. What percentage of this variance, then, is accounted for by $r = +0.50$? This is easily calculated by taking the square of r and multiplying by 100: in this case 0.50^2 x $100 = 25$ per cent of the total variance. This means that even if there were no individual differences in intelligence, the actual variance in school performance would still be 75 per cent of what it is when there *are* individual differences in intelligence. Again, even if the value of r between intelligence and attainment were to run as high as $+0.70$ (intelligence thus accounting for approximately 50 per cent of the variance in attainment), 50 per cent of the variance in attainment would still be unaccounted for.

A significant percentage of the variance in attainment must therefore be accounted for by qualities other than intelligence. This provides the point of departure for seeking correlates between personality variables and achievement in school. However, it must be emphasised that r is solely a quantitative index of the *degree of relationship* between two variables, and therefore this is the *only* inference we can draw from the value of r itself. We cannot infer that such a relationship is a causal one, even though it may be the case that some correlations do in fact reflect causal relations. Causal relations are always directional —the cause always precedes the effect—whereas correlations are not. As we shall see in Chapters 5 and 6, there is some evidence that extraverted children tend to perform better in primary school than introverts, that is, extraversion and performance are positively correlated. We are not able to say, however, that extraversion causes this better performance. We might hypothesise, for example, that at this level of education teachers tend to prefer extraverts, possibly because of the extravert's more manifest social orientation. This preference might cause teachers to reinforce the academic behaviour of extraverts with greater frequency and strength. If this hypothesis were true, the causal explanation of the correlation between extraversion and performance would be in terms of teachers' reinforcements of extraverts' academic behaviour. But the correlation alone has no bearing on the truth of this hypothesis.

The question of causality is a difficult one, but correlations do enable us to make predictions. If the correlation between extraversion and performance is significant and reliable we are able to predict that extraverts will tend to perform better than introverts. We are also able to predict that better performers will tend to be extraverts. It is these kinds of predictions that most of the studies of the relations between personality variables and attainment establish by the use of the correlation coefficients. However, these predictions do not establish the causes of performance, and this psychological task still lies ahead.

In the next chapter we shall consider the problem of discrepant achievement. This is an important focus of concern for educators, but it is an area that contains both logical and practical difficulties. However, a consideration of these difficulties will highlight the complex nature of the determinants of achievement.

References

[1] H. J. EYSENCK, *The Biological Basis of Personality*, Charles C. Thomas, Springfield, 1967.

[2] R. B. CATTELL, *The Scientific Analysis of Personality*, Penguin, Harmondsworth, 1965.

[3] C. BURT, "The Genetic Determination of Differences in Intelligence: A Study of Monozygotic Twins Reared Together and Apart", *British Journal of Psychology*, 1966, **57**, pp. 137-153.

[4] C. D. SPIELBERGER, "Theory and Research on Anxiety", in C. D. Spielberger (Ed.), *Anxiety and Behaviour*, Academic Press, New York, 1966.

[5] E. GAUDRY and C. D. SPIELBERGER, *Anxiety and Educational Achievement*, John Wiley & Sons, Sydney, 1971.

[6] C. S. HALL and G. LINDZEY, *Theories of Personality*, John Wiley & Sons, New York, 1957.

[7] L. J. BISCHOF, *Interpreting Personality Theories*, Harper & Row, New York, 1964.

[8] L. A. PERVIN, *Personality: Theory, Assessment and Research*, John Wiley & Sons, New York, 1970.

[9] H. J. EYSENCK, *Manual of the Maudsley Personality Inventory*, University of London Press, London, 1959.

[10] R. B. CATTELL and H. W. EBER, *Manual for Forms A and B Sixteen Personality Factor Questionnaire*, Institute for Personality and Ability Testing, Champaign, 1962.

[11] K. MacCORQUODALE and P. E. MEEHL, "On a Distinction between Hypothetical Constructs and Intervening Variables", *Psychological Review*, 1948, **55**, pp. 95-107.

[12] W. M. O'NEIL, "Hypothetical Terms and Relations in Psychological Theorizing", *British Journal of Psychology*, 1953, **44**, pp. 211-220.

[13] J. R. MAZE, "Do Intervening Variables Intervene?", *Psychological Review*, 1954, **61**, pp. 226-34.

[14] W. W. MEISSNER, "Intervening Constructs—Dimensions of Controversy", *Psychological Review*, 1960, **67**, pp. 51-72.

[15] R. McLAUGHLIN and R. PRECIANS, "Educational Psychology: Some Questions of Status", R. J. W. Selleck (Ed.), *Melbourne Studies in Education*, Melbourne University Press, Melbourne, 1969.

[16] F. D. NAYLOR, "Some Problems in the Relation between Psychology and Educational Psychology", *Educational Philosophy and Theory*, 1971, **3**, pp. 47-53.

[17] F. N. KERLINGER, *The Foundations of Behavioral Research: Educational and Psychological Inquiry*, Holt, Rinehart and Winston, New York, 1965.

[18] R. D. SAVAGE, "Personality Factors and Academic Performance", *British Journal of Educational Psychology*, 1962, **32**, pp. 251-53.

[19] R. D. SAVAGE, "Personality Factors and Academic Attainment in Junior School Children", *British Journal of Educational Psychology*, 1966, **36**, pp. 91-92.

[20] L. J. CRONBACH, *Essentials of Psychological Testing*, Harper & Row, New York; 2nd ed., 1960.

[21] P. E. VERNON, *Personality Assessment: A Critical Survey*, Methuen, London, 1964.

[22] R. B. CATTELL and M. D. L. CATTELL, *Handbook for the Junior-Senior High School Personality Questionnaire*, Institute for Personality and Ability Testing, Champaign, 1969.

[23] H. J. EYSENCK and S. B. G. EYSENCK, *Manual of the Eysenck Personality Inventory*, University of London Press, London, 1964.

[24] A. L. EDWARDS, *The Social Desirability Variable in Personality Assessment and Research*, Dryden Press, New York, 1957.

[25] A. L. EDWARDS, *Manual, Edwards Personal Preference Schedule*, Psychological Corporation, New York, 1959.

[26] J. ZUBIN, "Failures of the Rorschach Technique", *Journal of Projective Techniques*, 1954, **3**, pp. 303-15.

[27] H. J. EYSENCK, "A Rational System of Diagnosis and Therapy in Mental Illness", in *Progress in Clinical Psychology*, Vol. IV, Grune and Stratton, New York, 1960.

[28] F. N. COX, "Academic and Social Adjustment in 5th Grade Boys", *Australian Journal of Education*, 1961, **5**, pp. 185-92.

[29] C. E. OSGOOD, G. SUCI and P. TANNENBAUM, *The Measurement of Meaning*, University of Illinois Press, Urbana, 1957.

[30] J. C. NUNNALLY, *Psychometric Theory*, McGraw-Hill, New York, 1967.

[31] H. J. BUTCHER, *Human Intelligence, Its Nature and Assessment*, Methuen, London, 1968.

Chapter 2

The Problem of
Discrepant Achievement

One of the most important concerns of education is to ensure that each child is able to make the most of his abilities. The relation between intelligence and attainment is well known among teachers and well established in research. We might be tempted to believe that there the story ends, or should end, if an education system is doing its job properly. However, the relation between intelligence and attainment is far from perfect. If it were perfect the correlation between them would be unity ($r = 1 \cdot 00$). In fact the correlation is never unity; and on that account we will look more closely at the relation between other individual differences and attainment in order to appreciate some of the reasons for this.

School children who achieve below the level which is expected of them have attracted a great deal of research attention. The underachiever is a child with whom most teachers are very familiar. Failure to achieve in accordance with expectations, particularly when expectations exceed the actual achievement, is frequently attributed to aspects of "personality" or "character" believed to be important in performance. Such characteristics as lack of diligence and attentiveness are customarily regarded as important factors in determining performance, and their lack is frequently considered by teachers to be a valid reason for underachievement. However, underachievement is not necessarily such a simple and obvious matter. It depends on assumptions concerning the level of *possible* performance, and these assumptions are generally derived from the findings concerning the relation between ability and performance.

For both the teacher and the psychologist the underachieving child is one whose actual achievement, as indicated by his scholastic attainments in school, does not measure up to his potential achievement, as indicated by his abilities. This reflects the fact that there is not a perfect positive correlation between ability and attainment; but perhaps the concept of underachievement suggests that there ought to be or could be, "all other things being equal". In fact, however, all other things are never equal, which is to say that there are real and pervasive differences between people, in addition to differences in ability.

Nevertheless it might be the case that some of these are remediable, are subject to change in circumstances which differ from the usual, or even lose their potency when circumstances change.

Changes in the Effects of "Fixed" Characteristics

Classroom behaviour, including attainment, has a multiplicity of causes, some of which express an interaction of pupil and teacher characteristics. Many of these characteristics can be regarded as "fixed". This means that such characteristics are not of themselves capable of change, but the behaviour to which they lead might be affected by different circumstances. Sex is a biologically fixed characteristic, though of course the behaviours to which it leads might be susceptible to change. The differences between the sexes in various aspects of school performance have led Meyer and Thompson[1] to suggest that perhaps boys dislike school more than girls. The question is whether such differences are due to constitutional sex differences, or whether the differing social roles which are ascribed to the sexes are the predominating influence. Meyer and Thompson carried out a study designed to investigate whether female teachers showed differential approval and disapproval of the behaviour of male and female pupils. Their results indicated that male pupils received a higher incidence of teacher disapproval than female pupils, and that the boys were aware of this. They suggest that this arises from the implicit acceptance by the female teacher of feminine norms as appropriate for assessing classroom behaviour. Because of the nature of the female social role, girls' behaviour is more in conformity with such norms than boys' behaviour, and therefore the girls' behaviour is less "noticeable". Meyer and Thompson are suggesting that differential treatment of boys and girls by female teachers might well have effects on attainment levels which are quite independent of constitutional sex differences. When one considers that there is no evidence of sex differences in intelligence (Scottish Council for Research in Education[2]), differences between boys and girls in conduct and performance in school have to be accounted for in other terms. Thus, even "fixed" pupil characteristics, such as sex, do not inevitably lead to differential performance characteristics between boys and girls. Certainly other characteristics of the learning environment, such as the sex of the teacher and its implied attitudes and platitudes, interact with the sex of the pupil and influence attainment.

Evidence of this influence at more than one age level, suggests that it is widespread, particularly, it is assumed, where the greater proportion of teachers is female. In a study of sex differences in the reading performance of pupils taught by programmed instruction and others taught by female teachers, the investigator (J. D. McNeil, quoted in Schramm,[3] pp. 82-83) found that such differences did exist. Boys performed better than girls under programmed instruction, whereas girls performed better than boys in the classroom with a female teacher. We still do not know why boys' reading performance is better than girls' when they are taught through an apparently sexless medium;

but the effect of a female teacher is well established. In an earlier article, McNeil[4] revealed that the programme instructions were given in a male voice. This is of interest in relation to the subsequent advantage which the boys showed in performance, but we are not able to assess its significance.

The foregoing has illustrated that even fixed pupil characteristics do not necessarily have fixed effects on achievement. The programmed instruction example illustrates that a change in the medium of instruction can produce quite a dramatic change in the performance of males and females. The Meyer and Thompson study shows that some female teachers, at least, treat the behaviour of boys with more disapproval than that of girls. Since school organisation and functioning, unlike sex, are not fixed, the practical possibility of changing it in ways which will minimise sex differences in pupil performance is quite open.

Sex is an obvious personal attribute and a constant personal quality. Some personality attributes are regarded as being fixed in that, like sex, they are assumed to be genetically based. Burt[5] has assembled an impressive array of evidence that intelligence is largely dependent on genetic constitution, and this bears on the problem of underachievement. Presumably intelligence places a ceiling on performance, and the under-achiever is thereby the pupil who fails to reach that ceiling. Even here, however, teacher expectancies appear to intrude in a way which enables the ceiling to be raised, at least in so far as that ceiling is indicated by IQ.

Rosenthal and Jacobson[6] (Part II, Chapter 8) carried out a study which has important implications for the determinant role which teacher expectations play in the performance of school pupils. Basically they were interested in what has come to be called the "self-fulfilling prophecy" in an educational context. Specifically they were interested in finding out whether information given to teachers about pupils was related to changes in subsequent pupil performance. Rosenthal and Fode[7] had already demonstrated that experimenters using animal subjects in behavioural research could produce effects on an animal's performance as a result of false beliefs concerning the animal's characteristics. Thus animals characterised as "maze-bright" tended to perform better in experiments than those labelled "maze-dull", even though there was no basis in fact for such a distinction. The interesting question was whether in an analogous educational setting a teacher's expectation of a child's intellectual performance would serve as a self-fulfilling prophecy.

An intelligence test, purported to be a "test for intellectual blooming", was administered to all the children in an elementary school. Teachers were told that some of these children would show unusual intellectual growth during the school year. These comprised 20 per cent of the children tested, but they were actually selected by a table of random numbers so that in fact there was no reason to believe that such blooming would occur. This then was the experimental group who had been identified to their teachers as children who would show intellectual growth. The remaining 80 per cent constituted a control group since no false expectations concerning them were given to their teachers.

Eight months later all the children were retested on the same intelligence test and a gain score was calculated. The significant results are shown in Table 2.1.

TABLE 2.1

Mean Gains in IQ for Children in Grades 1 and 2 *

Grade	Control N	Control Mean	Experimental N	Experimental Mean	Difference	t	p
1	48	12·0	7	27·4	15·4	2·97	0·002
2	47	7·0	12	16·5	9·5	2·28	0·02

* Adapted from Rosenthal and Jacobson[6], Table 1.

Throughout the six grades in the elementary school both the experimental and control groups achieved gains in IQ over the eight-month test-retest period. However, as Table 2.1 reveals, in Grades 1 and 2 the differences in gains between the two groups was significantly in favour of the experimental group. In Grade I the experimental group gained 15·4 points in IQ, while in Grade 2 the gain was 9·5 points. The significance of the gain is expressed statistically by t and its probability by p (where probability values are below 0·05 they are by convention regarded as "significant").

Further studies concerning these data are reported in Rosenthal and Jacobson.[8] In a review of these studies Thorndike[9] points out that the data are not sufficient to sustain the authors' conclusions concerning teacher expectations as self-fulfilling prophecies. These criticisms are well-founded, and therefore the results reported in Table 2.1 should be regarded as indicating a *possible* effect of teacher expectations rather than being a conclusive demonstration. It is clear, however, that Rosenthal and Jacobson's data do not rule out the possibility of teacher expectations becoming self-fulfilling prophecies.

Defining Under- and Overachievement

Lavin[10] points out that the labelling of some school performances as underachievement or overachievement unfortunately tends to suggest that ability is the sole basis for predicting achievement. That an estimate of ability is a necessary piece of information is beyond dispute; but that it is an inaccurate predictor is also beyond question. Given this inaccuracy in prediction we should not be surprised to find wide individual differences in performance at the same ability level. The suggestion that ability level, or at least its measurement, may be subject to change as a function of teacher expectation, introduces a further complication into an already burgeoning complex.

These considerations suggest that the so-called fact of underachievement might itself be suspect. In calling a particular performance underachievement we must be careful not to beg questions concerning the real determinants of that performance. In a study by Carmical[11] an attempt was made to discriminate normal achievers and underachievers in terms of aptitudes, vocational preferences, values and temperament.

He defined an underachiever as a pupil whose IQ on the Otis Intelligence Test was between 110-125 and whose scholastic ranks were in the limits 2·0 to 2·9 (apparently within a total performance range of 2·0 to 5·0). In his results he found that his two groups were significantly differentiated on the verbal and numerical ability subtests of the Differential Aptitude Tests. As the authors of the manual for those tests have pointed out (Bennett, Seashore and Wesman[12]), scores on them correlate highly with scores on other standard intelligence tests. In another study of underachievement, Payne[13] used the verbal reasoning subscale of the Differential Aptitude Tests as the basis for defining his underachieving group. In these terms we can therefore see that the operational definitions of underachievement in these studies are not congruent, since part of the criterion for it in Payne's case becomes a distinguishing characteristic in Carmical's. If two cars of the same mechanical specifications perform differently on a hill climb then this difference cannot be accounted for in terms of mechanical specifications. If, on the other hand, their mechanical specifications had actually differed, this might be sufficient to account for their differences in performance. To pursue this analogy, Payne's subjects were similar in predicted performance ("mechanical specifications") whereas Carmical's subjects were different—and their performance in his study was in accordance with those differences. Carmical's results suggest that in fact he was not dealing with ordinary achievers and underachievers, but with high and low achievers; and it is well known that they can be differentiated in terms of intelligence.

The logical problems in the notion of underachievement are reflected in the concept of overachievement. In general, overachievers are defined as pupils whose school attainment is in excess of expectations formed on the basis of their ability. In this case obviously we would not say that such pupils ought to be performing in accordance with their ability, since an overriding concern of both teachers and psychologists is the maximisation of performance. But the concept of overachievement does suggest that there are variables in addition to ability which have positive effects on performance. This leads into the question of characterising the variables, and discovering whether they are absent in underachievers and whether underachievers possess characteristics which are absent in overachievers. If any of these characteristics are "fixed" in the sense that variables such as sex and intelligence might be regarded as fixed, perhaps their effects on school performance might remain fairly constant where school organisation is unable to take into account individual differences in the possession of these characteristics.

A Suggested Theory of Under- and Overachievement

Taylor[14] reviewed the relationship between certain hypothesised personality traits and discrepant achievement. He suggested that there were seven "traits" which were significantly related to achievement: (1) the overachiever has less anxiety than the underachiever and has greater self-control which would enable him to direct his anxiety to constructive ends; (2) the overachiever has positive feelings of self-worth whereas the underachiever is poorly adjusted and lacks self-confidence; (3) conformity to authority is more characteristic of the overachiever than the underachiever; (4) the overachiever is more concerned with social acceptance than the underachiever, and tends to have positive relations with peers; (5) the overachiever tends to have less conflict over issues concerning dependence and independence than the underachiever; (6) the overachiever is academically rather than than socially oriented in his activities; (7) the overachiever is more realistic in his choice of goals than the underachiever. Even though these were Taylor's general conclusions he pointed out that in many cases the evidence was ambiguous and sometimes contradictory.

Using the seven theoretical distinctions between under- and over-achievers proposed by Taylor[14] as a point of departure, Taylor and Farquar[15] found that it was possible to discriminate male and female Grade 11 students in relation to the theoretical constructs. Sex differences in responses to the Human Trait Inventory emerged from a factor analysis of the correlations between the items, which was performed for each sex separately. Table 2.2 shows the relationship between the extracted factors and the theoretical constructs.

TABLE 2.2
Graphic Relationship between Extracted and Theorised Constructs *

Extracted factors Males	Theorised constructs	Extracted factors Females
Agitation ⟶	Academic anxiety ⟵	Fantasy / Emotional instability
Academic compulsivity / Academic negativism ⟶	Activity patterns ⟵	Academic compulsivity
Ambivalence ⟶	Goal orientation	
Extrapunitive ⟶	Authority relations ⟵	Conservatism
Success orientation ⟶	Self-value	
	Interpersonal relations ⟵	Social distance
	Independence-dependence conflict	

* From Taylor and Farquar[15], p. 191.

The results suggested that among discrepant achievers anxiety manifests itself differently between the sexes. The factor connoted restlessness and tension among boys ("agitation"), whereas for girls it involved two distinct aspects: withdrawal into "fantasy" and acting-out behaviour ("emotional instability"). In their activity patterns both males and females were characterised by planning and organisation ("academic compulsivity"); but boys also possessed tendencies to reject school and showed little academic interest ("academic negativism"). Boys were ambivalent in their goal orientation, which suggests an underlying tension resulting from lack of purpose. They also tended to rebel against authority and social norms ("extrapunitive"), while girls expressed more concern with the maintenance of standards ("conservatism"). Boys showed a success orientation which placed a high value on self. Girls showed low involvement in interpersonal relations ("social distance"). None of the extracted factors appeared to be related to conflict over dependence and independence.

Thus the patterns of relationship differed between the sexes: six empirical factors for boys related to five of the theoretical constructs; and five empirical factors for girls related to four of the theoretical constructs. This kind of analysis, however, is confusing in terms of the original theoretical analysis (Taylor[14]). There the distinction being established was between under-and overachievers, the suggestion being that they were polarised with respect to the seven hypothesised traits. Since over- and underachievers were the subjects of the Taylor and Farquar study, the relation between the empirical factors derived from those groups and the theoretical constructs would have been of more relevant interest than sex differences. The combination of the two groups within sexes obscures the important distinction with which Taylor was originally concerned.

The distinction between overachievement and underachievement is significant and important in an educational context on two grounds. First, the facts of such achievement indicate the limits which measures of ability possess as predictors of performance. Underachievement suggests that a potential indicated by ability is not being realised, and that the factors which militate against its realisation require explication. Second, the fact of overachievement—performance in excess of expectations based on measured ability—indicates that an inevitable or necessary ceiling on performance is not dictated by ability levels. The warning of Lavin[10] is salutary. The assumption that a level of performance is an inevitable predicate of a level of ability renders underachievement mysterious and overachievement miraculous. The terms which refer to discrepant achievement are therefore highly relative. As indicated previously, the actual determinants of performance are complex and multiple; and the best single predictor of school performance —intelligence—does not thereby constitute the best explanation of it. So-called discrepant achievement will therefore be explained in terms which reflect this complexity and multiplicity, if it is ever to be explained at all.

Descriptive labels such as underachievement and overachievement are used where the determinants of performance other than intelligence are unknown or obscure. Such descriptive terms, however, can mislead us if we assume that they refer to an ideal performance level; such an assumption begs the question of what the *actual* determinants of performance are, because it suggests that determinants other than intelligence are in some sense "unreal". "Underachievement" and "overachievement" are relative to predictions from intelligence, and such predictions have no logical priority over any others. It is possible to predict performance from any variable which correlates with it. Relative to such a variable, pupils who exceeded the predicted performance would be "overachievers", while those whose performance was less than that predicted would be "underachievers". On this account we should constantly bear in mind that the discrepant achievement notions of underachievement and overachievement, as they are used in the literature, are relative to predictions based on intelligence. It is permissible to seek correlates of such discrepant achievement as a step towards accounting for the discrepancy. It was pointed out in Chapter I that we are not able to *infer* causes from correlations, though it is always possible that they *indicate* causes. However, correlational studies can stand as a descriptive account of a particular situation.

Some Personality Correlates of Discrepant Achievement

One study which sets out to achieve a description of the personality correlates of discrepant achievement is that of Oakland[16] (Part II, Chapter 9). He cites a review of Raph and Tannenbaum[17] concerning underachievement in which the authors refer to the inconclusive and conflicting findings of studies in the area. The more recent review by Taylor[14] suggests similar confusion. Oakland[16] held two factors responsible for this: inadequate experimental design and poor measures of personality traits. Oakland's study is a correlational study, which is to say that he is concerned to establish the relation between two sets of variables: personality and academic achievement. Personality he defines as the responses to the Edwards Personality Inventory (Edwards[18]); academic achievement is defined as the discrepancy between actual

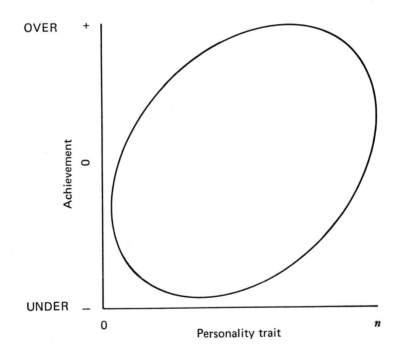

Fig. 2.1 The disposition of scores in a positive correlation.

and predicted performance, both expressed in terms of overall grade point average (GPA). In Chapter 1 some of the graphical characteristics of the correlation coefficient were described, and perhaps Oakland's results will mean more to students if we show the form of their graphical representation (Fig. 2.1). On the personality coordinate are the scores on a particular personality characteristic in ascending order of magnitude. On the achievement coordinate we have achievement scores, progressing from minus (where predicted GPA exceeds obtained GPA) through zero to plus (where predicted GPA is less than the obtained GPA). For positive values of Oakland's obtained correlation coefficients we can see from the disposition of the ellipse in Fig. 2.1 how increases in the scores on both variables tend to go along together. Figure 2.2 represents the situation where Oakland's correlation coefficients have negative values.

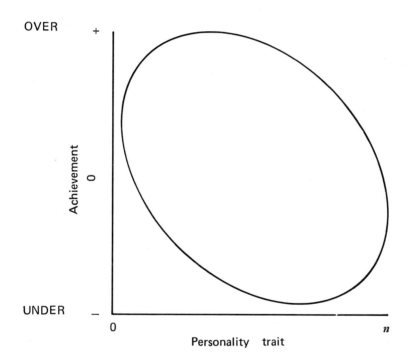

Fig. 2.2 The disposition of scores in a negative correlation.

Here we can see how increases in the score on one variable tend to go along with decreases in score on the other.

Although the magnitude of many of Oakland's correlation coefficients is quite high, he has protected himself against overgenerous interpretation and generalisation by setting a stringent significance level ($p < 0.01$). The more stringent the p level set, the less likely it is that an investigator will accept as significant those results which are due to chance. In his paper Oakland explains why he has set such a stringent level in his own results: "the large number of variables involved in this study made it more likely that some variables would reach significance by chance" (Oakland,[16] p. 454). A $p < 0.01$ means that there is less than one chance in 100 that the obtained value is not significantly different from zero. Table 2.3 summarises Oakland's significant results. Over- and underachievement were correlated with 53 scales from the Edwards Personality Inventory, and correlations with 19 of the scales were significant at the 0.01 level. Separate correlations were reported for each sex, and for high- and low-aptitude pupils within each sex. Oakland's discussion referred to the coherence with which certain of the scales cluster, and certainly one can see some conceptual relationship between these clusters and the results reported by Taylor and Farquar.[15] However, it should be borne in mind that these clusters are strictly hypothetical in that they are constituted by Oakland's own

TABLE 2.3

Significant Correlations ($p<0.01$) between Personality Characteristics and Over- and Underachievement *

| | | Males | | | Females | |
| | | | High | Low | | High | Low |
Characteristic	Total	Aptitude	Aptitude	Total	Aptitude	Aptitude
A 1. Plans and organises	0·471	0·496	0·446	0·262		0·322
2. Intellectually oriented	0·294					
3. Persistent	0·365		0·444			
4. Self-confident	0·314					
8. Conformity	0·260			0·215		
9. Leadership	0·329					
12. Impulsive				−0·249		
C 2. Avoids facing problems	−0·318			−0·240		
3. Perfectionist	0·501	0·497	0·494	0·239		0·362
4. Absent-minded				−0·250		−0·343
D 1. Motivated to succeed	0·463		0·568			
4. Plans work efficiently	0·522	0·536	0·507	0·347		0·396
5. Co-operate with a group	0·411		0·461			
6. Competitive	0·404	0·404	0·409			
9. To be logical	0·262		0·373			
10. To assume responsibility	0·427	0·400	0·442			
14. To be a dependable worker	0·435	0·453	0·436	0·282		0·401
E 2. To be critical of others				−0·264		−0·337
5. To become angry				−0·207		
8. To understand oneself	0·335		0·428			

* Adapted from Oakland[16], Table 2.

interpretation of his data. Other interpretations are certainly permissible. It would be possible to test Oakland's hypotheses, using factor analysis (see Chapter 4). If his interpretations are substantial it would be expected that factors would emerge from such an analysis in line with those interpretations. Meanwhile the congruence with Taylor and Farquar[15] is of interest, but its significance remains hypothetical.

A well-organised orientation to schoolwork was significantly correlated with achievement, but the correlations indicate that this characteristic pervaded non-academic areas as well. From Table 2.3 we can see that the scales A1, C3, D4, D9, and D14 do indicate a broadly generalised life style of personal organisation which goes beyond schoolwork. This combination of personality characteristics is similar to the "academic compulsivity" factor of Taylor and Farquar[15] but goes beyond the academic focus in that factor.

A second group of characteristics which was positively correlated with discrepant achievement appears to possess a strong attitudinal component. It may bear some relation to Taylor and Farquar's "success orientation" factor. Scales A3, A4, A9, D1, D6, and D10 do suggest an orientation towards achievement. As with Taylor and Farquar's "success orientation" factor, Oakland's correlations between scales and achievement were confined to the male sample. Oakland suggested that his result might reflect the differing social roles ascribed to males and females with regard to success orientation.

Traits relating to cooperation and conformity (A8, D5) were also positively correlated with discrepant achievement. Oakland suggested that such pupils were probably more appreciated by teachers, and this may have influenced the grades which such pupils received.

Oakland's results revealed few negative correlations between personality characteristics and discrepant achievement. For both males and females the underachiever tended to avoid facing problems (C2) more than the overachiever. The remaining negative correlations applied only to females. Female underachievers tended to be more absent-minded (C4), which is reminiscent of the female "fantasy" factor referred to by Taylor and Farquar.[15] Female underachievers also tended to become more angry and critical of others (E5, E2). There were no significant correlations between the personality scales and discrepant achievement for the high-aptitude females. This is surprising and difficult to account for. It may be that the personality scales measured by the inventory reflect traits that are predominantly "masculine". Certainly this result indicates the need for a more exhaustive search for correlates.

The most surprising result, however, was the lack of correlates which might be regarded as debilitating in some way. No variables connoting emotional instability such as anxiety about competition or conflict over dependency, showed significant correlations with discrepant achievement. As Oakland[16] points out, this suggests that they may be less important than the relative absence of constructive approaches to schoolwork by the underachiever.

Many features of Oakland's paper are noteworthy. First, there were sex differences in the results in that males achieved a greater number of significant correlation coefficients than females. No reasons for this can be inferred from the results themselves, which means that statements concerning the relation between personality characteristics and discrepant achievement have to be made with a sex qualification. The lack of consistency between the two ability levels indicates in some cases that the results must be qualified by reference to ability. There is a patent need for replication of the study in order to establish empirically the sex difference, and the reliability of the results. If the results are reliable, then, as Thorndike[19] suggests, it serves as "an important first step to understanding causes" (Oakland,[16] p. 457).

Second, it should be noted that Oakland's study purports to be no more than this. It is a ground-clearing exercise to establish the relations which subsequently will have to be explained. Since explanations are causal they cannot be inferred from Oakland's descriptive study; but such descriptions are invaluable in determining just what the phenomena are which the psychologist will have to explain.

In terms of the studies reviewed here, it is clear that the individual differences in school achievement cannot be reduced to individual differences in the intelligence of pupils. We have seen that performance may be affected by the sex of the teacher (Meyer and Thompson;[1] McNeil[4]) and expectations concerning performance (Rosenthal and Jacobson[6]). Since the notion of discrepant achievement is relative to achievement predicted from intelligence, we must be careful not to mislead ourselves into believing that for each child there is an inevitable or necessary level of performance. Our knowledge does not extend so far. Seeking the correlates of discrepant achievement is a first step to understanding causes, but it does not establish them. The study of Oakland[16] was concerned with establishing personality correlates of discrepant achievement; but it should be recognised that departures from predictions based on measured intelligence have no logical priority over other bases of prediction. As we shall see, other investigators are concerned with the predictive validity in their own right of other personality characteristics.

Those personality characteristics which do have facilitating or debilitating effects across the whole range of school achievement, if any do at all, cannot be determined by studies of underachievement and overachievement. Such studies are attempting to account for discrepant achievement—discrepant in the sense that it departs from predictions based on intelligence. Intelligence aside, however, it is conceivable that other personality characteristics have systematic effects on performance. Adjustment has been regarded as a global personality characteristic (e.g. Rogers[20,21,22]) which affects performance, and in the next chapter we will consider some theoretical problems concerning its definition and measurement, and some studies of its relation to attainment.

References

1 W. J. MEYER and G. C. THOMPSON, "Sex Differences in the Distribution of Teacher Approval and Disapproval Among Sixth Grade Children", *Journal of Educational Psychology*, 1959, **47**, pp. 385-96.

2 SCOTTISH COUNCIL FOR RESEARCH IN EDUCATION, *The Intelligence of Scottish Children*, University of London Press, London, 1933.

3 W. SCHRAMM, *The Research on Programmed Instruction, an Annotated Bibliography*, U.S. Office of Education, Washington D.C., 1964, p. 82.

4 J. D. MCNEIL, "Programmed Instruction as a Research Tool in Reading: An Annotated Case", *Journal of Programed Instruction*, 1962, **1**, pp. 37-42.

5 C. BURT, "The Genetic Determination of Differences in Intelligence: A Study of Monozygotic Twins Reared Together and Apart", *British Journal of Psychology*, 1966, **57**, pp. 137-53.

6 R. ROSENTHAL and L. JACOBSON, "Teachers' Expectancies: Determinants of Pupils' IQ Gains", *Psychological Reports*, 1966, **19**, pp. 115-18.

7 R. ROSENTHAL and K. L. FODE, "The Effect of Experimeter Bias on the Performance of the Albino Rat", *Behavioral Science*, 1963, **8**, pp. 183-89.

8 R. ROSENTHAL and L. JACOBSON, *Pygmalion in the Classroom, Teacher Expectation and Pupils' Intellectual Development*, Holt, Rinehart and Winston, New York, 1968.

9 R. L. THORNDIKE, "Review of Rosenthal and Jacobson, Pygmalion in the Classroom", *American Educational Research Journal*, 1968, **5**, pp. 708-11.

10 D. E. LAVIN, *The Prediction of Academic Performance*, Russell Sage Foundation, New York, 1965.

11 L. CARMICAL, "Characteristics of Achievers and Under-Achievers of a Large Senior High School", *Personnel and Guidance Journal*, 1964, **43**, pp. 390-95.

12 G. K. BENNETT, H. G. SEASHORE and A. G. WESMAN, *Manual for the Differential Aptitude Tests*, Forms L and M, Psychological Corporation, New York, 4th ed., 1966.

13 D. A. PAYNE, "The Concurrent and Predictive Validity of an Objective Measure of Academic Self-Concept", *Educational and Psychological Measurement*, 1962, **22**, pp. 773-80.

14 R. G. TAYLOR, "Personality Traits and Discrepant Achievement: A Review", *Journal of Counseling Psychology*, 1964, **11**, pp. 76-82.

15 R. G. TAYLOR and W. W. FARQUAR, "Personality, Motivation and Achievement: Theoretical Constructs and Empirical Factors", *Journal of Counseling Psychology*, 1965, **12**, pp. 186-91.

16 J. A. OAKLAND, "Measurement of Personality Correlates of Academic Achievement in High School Students", *Journal of Counseling Psychology*, 1969, **16**, pp. 452-57.

17 J. B. RAPH and A. TANNENBAUM, "Underachievement: Review of the Literature". Unpublished manuscript, 1961. Cited by A. T. Jersild, *The Psychology of Adolescence*, Macmillan, New York, 2nd ed., 1963.

18 A. L. EDWARDS, *Manual for the Edwards Personality Inventory*, Science Research, Chicago, 1968.

19 R. L. THORNDIKE, *The Concepts of Over and Under-Achievement*, Teachers College Press, Columbia University, New York, 1963.

20 C. R. ROGERS, *Client-Centered Therapy*, Houghton Mifflin, Boston, 1951.

21 C. R. ROGERS, *On Becoming a Person*, Constable, London, 1961.

22 C. R. ROGERS, *Freedom to Learn*, C. E. Merrill, Columbus, 1969.

Chapter 3

Adjustment and School Attainment

The relation between adjustment and attainment in school has not been clearly demonstrated. One reason for this is that many studies define adjustment in terms of measures of other psychological variables, whose relations with attainment are important in their own right. This suggests that adjustment may be redundant as a theoretical construct, since its meaning is reducible or equivalent to the meanings of other well developed constructs such as anxiety. In so far as adjustment is operationally defined in terms of, say, measures of anxiety, redundancy can be argued since adjustment clearly has no meaning which transcends the anxiety measure. However, it may be that adjustment can be more adequately conceptualised and defined in ways which would enable it to stand on its own theoretical feet, independently of other psychological constructs. An approach to adjustment through the study of the self-concept, and the relation of that concept to others, holds promise; and we will now consider how this approach might be made.

The self-concept is regarded as an important aspect of personality and a critical determinant of behaviour. Many psychological theorists place it in a central position in their theorising (e.g. Snygg and Combs,[1] Rogers,[2,3] Lewin,[4] Goldstein,[5] Maslow[6]) and although there is considerable difference between theories, they are substantially in agreement on the priority which they give to this concept. Self theories derive from the view that the individual's self-picture—the beliefs he has concerning his qualities, competence and shortcomings both as general phenomena and in particular cases—is an important determinant of his behaviour. So central is this view that the function of external agents as determinants of behaviour tends to be disregarded. The effects of the environment per se on the individual tend to be discounted in favour of the "phenomenal field" (Snygg and Combs[1]), the "life space" (Lewin[4]) and similar notions, which add up to the proposition that it is the world-as-perceived-and-understood which is crucial in accounting for the characteristics of behaviour. The self has two aspects which are related to this. First, our understanding of the world is a function, at least in part, of the distortions which our self-concept requires. Second, the self can also be an object of perception and understanding, and hence can itself be misperceived and misunderstood. In turn this leads to the distortion of experience. Rogers[2] provides the following example: "If the concept of the self includes the characteristic 'I am a poor student' the experience of receiving a high grade can be easily distorted to make it congruent with the self by perceiving in it such meanings as, 'That professor is a fool', 'It was just luck', etc." It may be, however, that "I am a poor student" was not a true characteristic, and to that extent both self and experience are misperceived and misunderstood.

Self-perception and self-understanding are frequently considered to be related to adjustment. Well-adjusted individuals are taken to be those whose self-perceptions are in accordance with their objective qualities, and who thereby lack the tensions generated by discrepancies between perceived and actual characteristics (Rogers[2]). This view implies no value judgements concerning the *actual* qualities of adjustment, because it allows differences between individuals in both self-perceptions and objective qualities. Adjustment in this context merely requires that these be congruent in the one person. This view takes adjustment to be a global phenomenon which affects every area of personal competence and thereby influences all aspects of behaviour. Such a notion, however, is not beyond theoretical criticism, in that adjustment can be regarded as being relative to particular situations. Thus a child might be regarded as adjusted in his home life but not in his school life. However, in order to show that home adjustment and school adjustment are theoretically distinct, we have to be sure that the measures used as operational definitions of these constructs necessarily imply such adjustments.

SOME CRITICISMS OF GLOBAL ADJUSTMENT

Cox[7] (Part II, Chapter 10), in an investigation of the relation between academic and social adjustment in 5th grade boys, concluded that they were independent of each other. Because this result conflicts with the results of American studies (e.g. Terman and Oden,[8] Buswell[9]), Cox suggested that there might be cultural differences between Australian children and Americans in the nature of their adjustments. More importantly, he suggested that the results are restricted to the measures used. Presumably, therefore, we can only compare the findings of different studies when we know that similar variables, measures and subject samples have been used. Cox used his results largely to argue against the concept of global or unitary adjustment on the grounds of the independence of academic and social adjustment. However it is not clear that the measures he used necessarily indicate such adjustments.

Table 3.1, reproduced from Cox's paper, shows the patterns of relationships between nine variables. These fall into two clusters which Cox interpreted as academic and social adjustment. Unfortunately, from this table we are only able to guess the quality of the relationships between the clusters; that is to say we cannot tell whether the correlation between any two variables is positive or negative. However, apart from this qualitative problem, it can be argued that the nine variables are

TABLE 3.1

Statistical Relationships between Measures of Academic and Social Adjustment *

	Academic adjustment					Social adjustment			
	Test anxiety	General anxiety	Achievement motive	Household duties	School marks	Attitudes to parents	Love	Sociometric status	Reputed immaturity
Academic adjustment:									
Test anxiety	—	XX	X	X	XX				
General anxiety	XX	—	XX		X				
Achievement motive	X	XX	—	XX	XX				
Household duties	X		XX	—	X				
School marks	XX	X	XX	X	—				
Social adjustment:									
Attitudes to parents						—	XX	XX	XX
Love						XX	—	X	XX
Social status						XX	X	—	XX
Reputed immaturity						XX	XX	XX	—

Notes: (a) X denotes statistical significance at 0·05 level.
(b) X X denotes statistical significance at 0·01 level.
(c) Absence of entries in upper right and lower left quadrants indicate independence of these measures of academic and social adjustment.
* From Cox⁷, Table I.

conceptually distinct from the construct of adjustment defined in terms of self. All five variables under academic adjustment index adherence to particular norms. This means that certain levels of anxiety, achievement motivation, participation in household tasks, and school marks are held to be predicates of academic adjustment. Similarly, certain attitudes to parents, the love they show for their children, the child's status in his peer group, and reputed immaturity by peers are held to be predicates of social adjustment. However, it should be noted that these characteristics are strictly only *imputed* to adjustment, and the fact that there are two clusters of correlations does not *show* that there are two areas of adjustment: it is just that they are *deemed* to be so. Depending on the signs of the correlation coefficients—positive or negative—one might regard the first cluster as, say, "motivation to achieve and conform"; and the second cluster as "social acceptance versus social rejection". The question is whether such characteristics are *necessary* to the concept of adjustment. Social acceptance on the one hand, and achievement, conformity and, say, low anxiety on the other, may reflect the adjustments of particular individuals, but their absence does not inevitably reveal lack of adjustment. It is not shown that social acceptability and adherence to achievement and conformity norms have necessary implications for the adjustment of the individual.

In Cox's terms we cannot refer to an individual's adjustment without making reference to the context to which he is adjusted. This makes adjustment relative to particular circumstances—family, school, peer group, and so on. The global adjustment position, as exemplified by

Rogers[2], implicitly asserts that adjustment is a general condition which enables the individual to cope with his life circumstances. The tenability of either position depends heavily on the measures which are used as operational definitions of adjustment. For example, use of an anxiety measure as an operational definition of adjustment, thereby suggesting that, say, low anxiety is indicative of good adjustment, ignores the possibility that on some occasions high anxiety may have facilitating effects (Alpert and Haber;[10] Gaudry and Spielberger[11]). Thus we have to be sure that the measures obtained are those required by the theory of adjustment. If they are not, they can throw no light on the question of the truth or falsity of the theory.

The importance of clarity, conciseness and logic in theorising is emphasised by Cox's argument. If the concept of adjustment—global or otherwise—is to have any scientific meaning, it must eventually imply observable consequences. Cox argued that his findings conflicted with the notion of global adjustment; but this may merely mean that because the concept is so vague and ill-defined, it is impossible to specify consequences with the precision which empirical tests require.

Cox[7] concluded: "at the present time . . . all-embracing generalisations about child adjustment are unlikely to have general validity" (p. 190). This conclusion may be increasingly valid as empirical research becomes increasingly remote from theories of adjustment. On these grounds there would seem to be some point in getting back to theory in order to see what direct operational consequences can be deduced.

ROGERS' THEORY OF ADJUSTMENT

Self-theorists who are concerned with the practice of psychotherapy, and in particular Rogers,[3,12,13] have amassed considerable evidence (Rogers and Dymond[14]) indicating that a discrepancy between the self-concept and experience, such that aspects of behaviour can be "disowned", is a significant feature of psychological disturbance. The well-adjusted person is regarded as one where such a discrepancy does not exist; where self and experience are said to be "congruent". Changes in the way a patient refers to himself are reported as therapy progresses, and these are held to indicate increasing congruence between self and experience. Self-statements also tend to become more positive, concentrating on constructive aspects of the person's personality, and so on. Rogers,[3] on the basis of his therapeutic experience and the research findings, has come to regard the self-concept as an important determinant of educational performance. He strongly subscribes to the notion of global adjustment and thereby regards a psychologically well-adjusted self as a necessary condition for the development of competence in the educational sphere.

Rogers' concept of adjustment is implicit in his formulations concerning the "fully functioning" person (Rogers[3]). He sees the production of such a person as being the end-point of any positive learning experience, whether this takes place in the context of psychotherapy or within a system of formal education. Such a person is said to manifest particular characteristics: he is open to experience (and thereby lacks the defences which distort it); he lives existentially (taking the most economic course to the satisfaction of his needs in the immediate situation); he feels secure about behaving in ways which "feel right" even though there is no conscious or rational basis for this behaviour at the time. The important feature of these characteristics is that they have no criteria which go beyond the individual, and hence they cannot be evaluated in terms of adherence to the norms of a particular culture or society, or in terms of scores on psychological tests which are normative in character. Thus Rogers is repudiating a notion of adjustment which is operationally defined in terms of such adherences or scores, and he explicitly states that the operational hypotheses "would be culture-free or universal . . . rather than being different for each culture" (Rogers[3] p. 289).

Definitions of adjustment which require the "well-adjusted" person to hold certain values, to adhere to the norms of a wider group, to be free from anxiety, and so on, conflict with Rogers' position because they are implicitly normative and involve the imposition of a concept of adjustment which is derived from a frame of reference external to any particular individual. A further consideration also applies here: such definitions imply that the construct of adjustment is reducible to other psychological variables or constructs such as values, anxieties and so on.

Studies of the Relationship between Adjustment and Achievement

Cox[7] argued against the concept of global adjustment on the grounds that academic and social adjustment were independent of each other in his results. Rogers[2,12,13] argued from data gathered during psychotherapy, a context rather different from that of education, for a concept of global adjustment, and its influence in education. Cox's findings reflect those reviewed by Donahue, Coombs and Travers[15] which suggested a pervasive zero relation between psychological adjustment and achievement.

However, more recent studies have reported positive relations between adjustment and attainment and this may reflect both better theorising and more appropriate operational definitions. Favourable self-perception seems to be closely related to personal adjustment (Wylie[16]), as does the degree of similarity between the self-concept and the concept of the ideal self (Rogers and Dymond;[14] Wylie[16]). A recent review of the relation between self-concept and school achievement (Purkey[17]) argued for a direct and positive relation between a favourable self-concept and performance; it held that the successful student sees himself in essentially positive ways.

Not all studies show this relationship to be maintained when the effects of other variables, and particularly intelligence, are accounted for. Matlin and Mendelsohn[18] (Part II, Chapter 11) obtained measures of personal and social adjustment from the California Test of Personality (CTP) for 68 Grade 5 children, and correlated them with two measures of achievement: performance on the Stanford Achievement Test Battery (SATB), and grades given by teachers. Table 3.2, taken from their paper, shows the correlations between achievement, adjustment and IQ. There are some interesting features in this table.

TABLE 3.2
Correlations Between All Variables †
(N — 68)

	IQ	Achievement (teachers' grades)	Achievement (test)	Personal adjustment	Social adjustment
IQ	—	0·60 * * *	0·59 * * *	0·33 * * *	0·32 * * *
Achievement (teachers' grades)		—	0·73 * * *	0·44 * * *	0·42 * * *
Achievement (test)			—	0·30 * *	0·26 *
Personal adjustment				—	0·68 * * *
Social adjustment					—

* Significant beyond 0·05 level of confidence.
** Significant beyond 0·02 level of confidence.
*** Significant beyond 0·01 level of confidence.
† From Matlin and Mendelsohn[18], Table I.

The correlation between personal and social adjustment is quite high (0·68), and their correlations with other variables are almost identical. This led Matlin and Mendelsohn to suggest that ". . . it is probably erroneous to assume that the two subtests are truly measuring different aspects of adjustment. Future researchers and users of the test (CTP) would probably be better advised to combine the sections into one general adjustment scale."

Table 3.3 shows the relations of adjustment to achievement when IQ is held constant. Here the correlations between adjustment measures and achievement measured by the SATB were no longer significant when the effects of IQ were accounted for.

TABLE 3.3
First-order Partial Correlations Between Achievement and Adjustment with IQ Held Constant *

	Achievement (test)	Achievement (teachers' grades)
Personal adjustment	0·14	0·32 * * *
Social adjustment	0·09	0·30 * *

** Significant beyond the 0·02 level of confidence.
*** Significant beyond the 0·01 level of confidence.
* From Matlin and Mendelsohn[18], Table 2.

However, the relations between adjustment and grades given by teachers were still significant. Matlin and Mendelsohn suggested that teachers might base their assessments on adjustment as well as accomplishment.

A study by Ringness[19] also used the CTP as an index of adjustment. Two groups of 30 bright Grade 9 boys, selected for high and low achievement, were compared on the CTP and two other measures of adjustment. No gross adjustment differences emerged. Both groups were similar in personal and social adjustment, as indicated by the CTP. The high achievers tended to have a more pronounced sense of personal worth, but they also showed more nervous symptoms. Their family relations and school relations tended to be more satisfactory. The other measures of adjustment—a sentence completion test and "A Self Test"—showed no differences between the two groups.

One problem with the CTP as a measure of adjustment is that it tends to depend on adherence to social norms as the criterion of adjustment. However, there are good reasons for treating conformity and adjustment as quite distinct aspects of personality. This becomes clear in circumstances where social norms are ambiguous, uncertain, or in flux. Thus we might require a "well-adjusted" person to "adhere to the law". But which law? The "law of the land" seems not to be a satisfactory answer. A person may adhere to traffic laws but smoke marijuana and be a draft dodger. To regard such a person as maladjusted is to make a value judgement from some preferred standpoint. It also ignores the fact that there is genuine dispute concerning the validity and morality of some laws, such as those which prohibit the use of marijuana and which enforce conscription for military service. This is not to argue that such a person is well-adjusted, but merely that the criteria for "adjustment" must be value-free if the term is to be of any use. If "adjustment" means "adherence to social norms" it would seem to be synonymous with conformity, and there is no point in continuing to use a psychological term if it is not distinct in meaning from other terms.

STUDIES USING "SELF" AND "IDEAL-SELF" DISCREPANCY AS A MEASURE OF ADJUSTMENT

Approaches to adjustment by means of the discrepancy between "self" and "ideal-self" ratings (Wylie[16]) holds promise for achieving an assessment of adjustment which is independent of conformity. Adjustment here is indicated by the degree of discrepancy: the smaller the discrepancy the better adjusted the person is held to be. A study by McCallon[20] used a 22-item rating scale of self and ideal-self as an index of adjustment. Self-ratings were prefaced by "I am . . .", and ideal-self ratings by "I would like to be . . .". The 22 adjectives used were: friendly, happy, kind, brave, honest, likeable, trusted, good, proud, lazy, loyal, cooperative, cheerful, thoughtful, popular, courteous, jealous, obedient, polite, bashful, clean, helpful. The response to each adjective was made in one of five categories: not at all, not very often, some of the time, most of the time, and all the time; and each was assigned a value from 1 to 5 depending on the response category. The discrepancy between the total scores for self and ideal-self was used as the index of adjustment. In Table 3.4, the mean self and ideal-self scores for three discrepancy groups—high, medium and low—are shown.

The similarity of the ideal-self ratings indicated by the means of the three groups led McCallon to suggest that the discrepancy scores

TABLE 3.4
Mean Self Rating and Ideal-Self Rating for Three
Discrepancy Groups *

Rating	High discrepancy	Median discrepancy	Low discrepancy
	N = 56	N = 82	N = 54
Self	72·56	87·78	101·23
Ideal-self	104·95	105·96	107·40

* Adapted from McCallon[20], Table 3 (p. 47).

merely reflected the status of the self-concept itself. The maximum possible score for each set of ratings is 110, and we can see that the ideal-self ratings in all three groups approach this maximum. This raises the possibility that the adjectives themselves suggest what an ideal-self ought to be like, and that the obtained responses were made in accordance with this normative stereotype. This could have produced an effect which was due to the social desirability of the adjectives. The work of Edwards[21] has indicated the need to control responses to personality measures for the effects of social desirability response sets. When items suggest a socially desirable response this is the response which tends to be made, according to Edwards' argument. If McCallon's ideal-self ratings were contaminated by social desirability response sets, the fact that the values for ideal-self approach the maximum possible one is understandable. This could also have obscured the true discrepancies between self and ideal-self ratings, since, logically, nothing requires the value of an ideal-self rating to approach the maximum.

Such ratings do not inevitably involve social desirability response sets. A study by Naylor and Gaudry[22] (Part II, Chapter 12) used an operational definition of adjustment which attempted (1) to accord with the essential elements of Rogers' construct (Rogers[3]), (2) to be non-normative in the sense that adjustment scores derived were independent of social norms, and (3) to be unaffected by social desirability response sets. Their measure of adjustment was derived from the semantic differential technique (Osgood, Suci and Tannenbaum[23]) which has been developed as a measure of meaning. Naylor and Gaudry argued that the relation between the *meanings* of "myself" and "the person I would like to be" to an individual was an appropriate index of the discrepancy between self and ideal-self in that individual. In order to place their argument in perspective, some of the characteristics of the semantic differential technique (*SD*) will be described.

The studies reported by Osgood, Suci and Tannenbaum,[23] and later studies reviewed by Osgood,[24] and Snider and Osgood,[25] indicated that a significant proportion of the meanings of different concepts could be described by three independent dimensions, which they labelled *evaluation, activity* and *potency*. Each dimension is defined by a set of bipolar adjectives, and the three labels are deemed to be the most appropriate terms summarising the common aspects of the bipolar adjectives on the dimension concerned. Thus an evaluative dimension is typically defined by such bipolarities as *good-bad, sweet-sour, glad-*

sad; an activity dimension by polarities like *fast-slow, hot-cold*; and a potency dimension by *strong-weak, large-small*. We will not be concerned here with the mathematics used to arrive at such dimensions, but interested students may refer to Osgood, Suci and Tannenbaum.[23] In so far as the meaning of any concept involves any of the dimensions, it can be located in a space which the dimensions define. The similarity in the meaning of any two concepts is indicated by the similarity of their locations in this space. A quantitative index of this similarity can be calculated, and this is referred to as a *D* (distance) score. The important feature of such meanings is that they can be quite idiosyncratic: the meaning of a particular concept can therefore differ from person to person, while the meaning of certain concepts *within the one person* can be quite similar. It is this similarity which the quantitative index (the *D* score) expresses.

The following simple example will make this point clear. John and Mary have been asked to rate the concepts "myself" and "the person I would like to be" on three bipolar adjectival scales, "good-bad", "sweet-sour" and "glad-sad". Their responses are as follows:

JOHN

MYSELF — THE PERSON I WOULD LIKE TO BE

good: : : : X : : bad (1 2 3 4 5)   good: X : : : : : bad (1 2 3 4 5)

sweet: : : : X : : sour (1 2 3 4 5)   sweet: : : X : : : sour (1 2 3 4 5)

glad: : X : : : : sad (1 2 3 4 5)   glad : : X : : : : sad (1 2 3 4 5)

MARY

MYSELF — THE PERSON I WOULD LIKE TO BE

good: : X : : : : bad (1 2 3 4 5)   good: X : : : : : bad (1 2 3 4 5)

sweet: : X : : : : sour (1 2 3 4 5)   sweet: : X : : : : sour (1 2 3 4 5)

glad: : : : X : : sad (1 2 3 4 5)   glad: X : : : : : sad (1 2 3 4 5)

We can see that John and Mary have rated both "myself" and "the person I would like to be" differently. We might therefore infer that these concepts mean different things to them. The generalised distance formula gives us a quantitative index of the relation between the meanings of the concepts separately for John and Mary. This formula is:

$$D = \sqrt{\Sigma d^2}$$

where D = distance between concepts,

Σ = the sum of

d^2 = squared difference between scales.

Applying this formula to the responses of John and Mary we get the following values of D:

John

$$D = \sqrt{3^2 + 1^2 + 0^2}$$
$$= \sqrt{10}$$
$$= 3\cdot16$$

Mary

$$D = \sqrt{1^2 + 0^2 + 3^2}$$
$$= \sqrt{10}$$
$$= 3\cdot16$$

Thus, even though the concepts have different meanings for John and Mary, the *relations* between the meanings *within* John and Mary individually are the same. For both of them, the discrepancy between self and ideal-self is the same, even though the meaning of these concepts to John and Mary is different.

The degree of similarity-dissimilarity in the meaning of the concepts "myself" and "the person I would like to be" was argued by Naylor and Gaudry[22] to be an adequate operational definition of Rogers' concept of adjustment (Rogers[3]). Greater similarity of meaning was held to reflect greater adequacy of adjustment.

The relation between adjustment so defined and performance in mathematics was the focal point of Naylor and Gaudry's investigation. They employed statistical controls for the effects of individual differences in intelligence, trait anxiety and test anxiety on mathematics performance, in order to ensure that the effects of these would not be confused with the effects of adjustment. The separate effects of these variables are indicated by the values of the adjusted mean scores for mathematics performance shown in Table 3.5. The adjusted mathematics means for the groups differed significantly.

TABLE 3.5
Unadjusted and Adjusted Mean Mathematics Scores for Large and Small Self-Ideal Self Discrepancies

Discrepancy between self and ideal self	Mean mathematics scores			
	Unadjusted	Adjusted for		
		Intelligence	Trait anxiety	Test anxiety
Large	48·78	49·52	48·97	49·19
Small	51·70	50·91	51·50	51·27

When the effects of intelligence were held constant the mean mathematics scores did come closer together, but the difference was still statistically significant. Thus it can be seen that the discrepancy between self and ideal-self was still significantly related to mathematics performance. A similar relationship was maintained when the effects of trait anxiety and anxiety about tests and test-like situations were also accounted for.

Naylor and Gaudry's results are important because the adjustment effect is maintained independently of the effects of the other individual differences. Their measure of adjustment was uncontaminated by moralistic judgements concerning the qualities which make it up, and therefore it was closer to Rogers' definition of adjustment than more normative measures. Their results also suggest that the concept of global adjustment, which is basic to Rogers' theory, may be theoretically viable in spite of the arguments of Cox.[7] Replication of Naylor and Gaudry's study over a wider age range, using other school subjects as criteria, would indicate the depth and range of their measure as an index of global adjustment and its relation to a wider range of school performance.

We have seen that assessing the relation between adjustment and school performance is not a straightforward matter. In theoretical terms it is not always clear what the concept of adjustment refers to, particularly when it is confused with other psychological variables such as anxiety and conformity. Rogers[3] argued for a notion of adjustment which was independent of adherence to social norms. Naylor and Gaudry[22] used this theoretical notion as the basis for their operational index of adjustment, which they found to be significantly related to performance in mathematics, independent of the effects of anxiety and intelligence. On this basis they argued that adjustment was a psychological construct which was distinct from other constructs, and which was therefore of theoretical importance in accounting for performance.

A study by Everett[26] (Part II, Chapter 13) has attempted a qualitative characterisation of the self-concepts of high, medium and low academic achievers. Semantic differential responses to 26 concepts on nine bipolar semantic scales were obtained from 59 female university students.

Clear differences between the three groups of achievers can be seen in the results (Table 3.6). High achievers clearly excluded the clinical concepts and two non-achievement related concepts ("skipping lectures"; "keeping irregular hours") from the self cluster. The remaining concepts tended to be oriented into a global self-configuration. By contrast, in the medium and low groups the self structure contained a much more restricted range of concepts. Medium and low achievers also incorporated the clinical concepts much more closely with the self structure. In the low achiever, "skipping lectures" and "keeping irregular hours" formed part of the self cluster. Interestingly, for the lower groups the concept "ideal student" was at the most remote point from "myself" and "me as a student", whereas among high achievers it was much closer to the self structure.

Everett's results are a significant and coherent descriptive account of the qualities of self-concepts at different levels of achievement. It was not his concern to discover whether these descriptions are indicative of a more general state of affairs. Nevertheless his study involved a new approach to the characterisation of self-concepts, and it will be left to further studies to indicate its breadth and scope.

In this chapter we have been considering one variable—adjustment—and its relation to achievement. This, however, is not the only possible

TABLE 3.6

Distances of Other Concepts from Self-Concept in Three Achievement Groups*

Achievement group	Near	Far
High	Myself Me as a student Non-conformity Authority Home Party-going Refectory Ideal student Pursuit of knowledge Discussion Initiative Private studying Career Marriage Love Sex Participation in societies Participation in sport Exams Ambition Competition	Frustration Guilt Anxiety Keeping irregular hours Skipping lectures
Medium	Myself Me as a student Private studying Party-going Non-conformity Refectory Keeping irregular hours Skipping lectures Anxiety Frustration Exams Guilt Authority	Marriage Sex Love Home Competition Ambition Pursuit of knowledge Initiative Discussion Career Participation in societies Participation in sport Ideal student
Low	Myself Me as a student Private studying Refectory Skipping lectures Keeping irregular hours Exams Anxiety Guilt Frustration Authority	Party-going Sex Love Home Competition Ambition Non-conformity Participation in societies Marriage Career Pursuit of knowledge Discussion Participation in sport Initiative Ideal student

* Estimated from Everett[26], Fig. I.

approach to the understanding and explanation of performance. The factor analytic study of personality (Cattell,[27] Eysenck and Eysenck[28]) attempts to achieve an exhaustive description of the variables which constitute personality. Studies of the relations of these variables to particular aspects of behaviour can take the variables separately, together as a group, or in interaction with one another. Since the factor analytic technique is basic to the definition of the personality variables, in the next chapter we will consider some of its psychological attributes. In subsequent chapters we will look at the relation between achievement and the personality variables so defined.

References

[1] D. SNYGG and A. COMBS, *Individual Behaviour*, Harper and Bros., New York, 1949.

[2] C. R. ROGERS, "A Theory of Therapy, Personality, and Interpersonal Relationships, as Developed in the Client-Centered Framework", in S. Koch (Ed.), *Psychology: A Study of a Science, Vol. III, Formulations of the Person and the Social Context*, McGraw-Hill, New York, 1959.

[3] C. R. ROGERS, *Freedom to Learn*, C. E. Merrill, Columbus, 1969.

[4] K. LEWIN, *A Dynamic Theory of Personality*, McGraw-Hill, New York, 1935.

[5] K. GOLDSTEIN, *Human Nature in the Light of Psychopathology*, Harvard University Press, Cambridge, Mass., 1940.

[6] A. H. MASLOW, *Motivation and Personality*, Harper & Row, New York, 1954.

[7] F. N. COX, "Academic and Social Adjustment in 5th Grade Boys", *Australian Journal of Education*, 1961, **5**, pp. 185-92.

[8] L. M. TERMAN and M. H. ODEN, *The Gifted Child Grows Up*, Stanford University Press, Stanford, 1947.

[9] M. BUSWELL, "The Relationship between the Social Structure of the Classroom and the Academic Success of the Pupils", *Journal of Experimental Education*, 1953, **22**, pp. 37-52.

[10] R. ALPERT and R. N. HABER, "Anxiety in Academic Achievement Situations", *Journal of Abnormal and Social Psychology*, 1960, **61**, pp. 207-15.

[11] E. GAUDRY and C. D. SPIELBERGER, *Anxiety and Educational Achievement*, John Wiley & Sons, Sydney, 1971.

[12] C. R. ROGERS, *Client-Centered Therapy*, Houghton Mifflin, Boston, 1951.

[13] C. R. ROGERS, *On Becoming a Person*, Constable, London, 1961.

[14] C. R. ROGERS and R. DYMOND, *Psychotherapy and Personality Change*, University of Chicago Press, Chicago, 1954.

[15] W. T. DONAHUE, C. H. COOMBS and R. W. M. TRAVERS, *The Measurement of Student Adjustment and Achievement*, University of Michigan Press, Ann Arbor, 1949.

[16] R. C. WYLIE, *The Self-Concept: A Critical Survey of Pertinent Research Literature*, University of Nebraska Press, Lincoln, 1961.

[17] W. W. PURKEY, *Self-Concept and School Achievement*, Prentice-Hall, Englewood Cliffs, 1970.

[18] A. H. MATLIN and F. A. MENDELSOHN, "The Relationship Between Personality and Achievement Variables in the Elementary School", *Journal of Educational Research*, 1965, **58**, pp. 457-59.

[19] T. A. RINGNESS, "Emotional Adjustment of Academically Successful and Nonsuccessful Bright Ninth Grade Boys", *Journal of Educational Research*, 1965, **59**, pp. 88-91.

[20] E. L. McCALLON, "Self-Ideal Discrepancy and the Correlates Sex and Academic Achievement", *Journal of Experimental Education*, 1967, **35**, pp. 45-49.

[21] A. L. EDWARDS, *The Social Desirability Variable in Personality Assessment and Research*, Dryden Press, New York, 1957.

[22] F. D. NAYLOR and E. GAUDRY, "The Relationship of Adjustment, Anxiety and Intelligence to Mathematics Performance", *Journal of Educational Research* (in press).

[23] C. E. OSGOOD, G. SUCI and P. TANNENBAUM, *The Measurement of Meaning*, University of Illinois Press, Urbana, 1957.

[24] C. E. OSGOOD, "Studies of the Generality of Affective Meaning Systems", *American Psychologist*, 1962, **17**, pp. 10-28.

[25] J. G. SNIDER and C. E. OSGOOD, *Semantic Differential Technique: A Source Book*, Aldine, Chicago, 1969.

[26] A. V. EVERETT, "The Self Concept of High, Medium and Low Academic Achievers", *Australian Journal of Education*, 1971, **15**, pp. 319-24.

[27] R. B. CATTELL, *The Scientific Analysis of Personality*, Penguin, Harmondsworth, 1965.

[28] H. J. EYSENCK and S. B. G. EYSENCK, *The Structure and Measurement of Personality*, Routledge and Kegan Paul, London, 1969.

Chapter 4

The Factor Analytic Approach
to the Study of Personality

Factor analysis is a mathematical technique which enables us to achieve a simplified description of complex data in mathematical terms. It has already been argued that personality is a very complex subject and therefore it may be that factor analysis could be used to achieve a method of describing in quantitative terms individual differences in personality characteristics (factors). It is the function of this chapter to indicate the nature of these descriptions in psychological terms, and hence we will not become involved with the mathematical methods whereby these descriptions are obtained. However, it will be necessary to describe some quantitative features of the description of personality by factor analytic methods.

Factor analysis generally starts with a matrix of correlation coefficients. We know that a correlation coefficient is a quantitative statement of relation between two variables. A matrix of correlation coefficients shows the correlations between every pair of variables in the matrix. Thus, if we have a 4×4 correlation matrix there will be 12 correlation coefficients contained within it. Table 4.1 shows a hypothetical example.

TABLE 4.I
A Hypothetical 4 x 4 Correlation Matrix

		Variable			
		1	2	3	4
Variable	1	—	0·53	—0·36	0·82
	2	0·53	—	0·16	—0·48
	3	—0·36	0·16	—	0·31
	4	0·82	—0·48	0·31	—

You will notice that the matrix is symmetrical about its diagonal, which is blank. Thus the columns below the diagonal contain the same values as the rows above the diagonal. The diagonals of the matrix are blank, but values have to be inserted before the matrix can be factor analysed. These are called *communality estimates*, and they can vary with the particular mathematical technique of factor analysis, and with the purposes for which the factor analysis is conducted. The details of this need not concern us here.

The number of factors which a factor analysis yields is never greater than the number of variables. Depending on the values of the correlation coefficients in the matrix, the number of factors is generally considerably less than the number of variables. From our hypothetical correlation matrix we would therefore obtain no more than four factors. After factor analysis each variable will have a value on one or more factors, and these values are referred to as *factor loadings*. Technically, factor loadings are the correlation of the variable with the factor, and, therefore, like the values of all correlation coefficients, they fall within the range $+1$ to -1.

It will be recalled that the percentage of variance accounted for by any particular correlation coefficient can be calculated by squaring the coefficient and multiplying the product by 100. This percentage is called the *common factor variance* of the two variables. The remainder of the variance is that which is specific to each variable. We know that the amount of variance in school performance accounted for by intelligence is about 25 per cent (Cattell;[1] Cattell, Sealey and Sweney[2]). The remaining 75 per cent is specific to school performance in that it is not accounted for by intelligence. However, this specificity should not be taken to imply uniqueness; it may be that the remaining 75 per cent can be accounted for by correlations with variables which are independent of both intelligence and each other. Such variables might include personality characteristics, motives, and so on. The factor analysis of the correlation coefficients between variables enables us to discover just how many independent characteristics (factors) are required to account for the observed correlations. They are the minimum number or most parsimonious set of independent dimensions which constitute a mathematical description.

Such a mathematical description has, of itself, no direct psychological implications. Such descriptions have to be interpreted in terms of the characteristics of the variables which load on the factors. In a sense this is going beyond the facts to a "construct" which is held to be the best characterisation of the obtained factor loadings in psychological terms. This is not always an easy or obvious thing to achieve, since the criteria for many characterisations are not precisely specified. It may not be going too far to assert that there is considerable art involved in achieving an appropriate characterisation. It would be possible, of course, to ignore such characterisations altogether and merely distinguish between factors by differential symbolic notation, for example, by calling one factor "*A*", another "*B*", and so on. This produces difficulties on a psychological level since it renders their theoretical implications obscure, thereby contributing little to psychological understanding. Constructs, therefore, are generally the psychological end-products of a factor analysis; but it is important to recognise that the factor analytic technique does not permit us to infer such constructs formally. Thus our constructs must be hypotheses or hunches. The arbitrariness of such characterisations depends on the arbitrariness of the psychological theory we might favour as a basis for our characterisations.

Consider the following hypothetical example. Let us suppose that we have obtained measures from a sample of secondary school pupils on the following six variables.

(1) mathematics performance,
(2) English performance,
(3) enthusiasm for cryptic crossword puzzles,
(4) enjoyment of sports,
(5) voluntary participation in school plays,
(6) enthusiasm for parties.

Let us suppose further that we have calculated correlation coefficients for each of these variables with each other, and factor analysed the obtained correlation matrix. The resulting hypothetical factor matrix is shown in Table 4.2.

TABLE 4.2
A Hypothetical Factor Matrix

Variable	Factor	
	X	Y
(1)	0·85	0·04
(2)	0·76	—0·09
(3)	0·88	0·00
(4)	0·07	0·91
(5)	—0·11	0·82
(6)	—0·02	0·87

How might we psychologically characterise factors X and Y? The factor loadings indicate that two clusters of variables respectively define factors X and Y. The first cluster (variables 1, 2 and 3) has large loadings on factor X and negligible loadings on factor Y; whereas the second cluster (variables 4, 5 and 6) has neglible loadings on factor X and large loadings on factor Y. The first factor (X) is therefore defined by performance in mathematics and English, and enthusiasm for cryptic crosswords. The second factor is defined by enjoyment of sports and parties, and participation in school plays. Can we find constructs which would psychologically characterise these definitions of the factors? Factor X is predominantly *cognitive* in its emphasis. It includes cognitive performances and enthusiasms, and it could therefore be regarded as a "cognitive orientation" factor. Each of the variables on factor Y involves interaction with others, either as competitors, players and audience, or mutual participation. Thus its emphasis is predominantly *social*, and it could therefore be regarded as a "social interaction" factor. In terms of their scores on the six variables, individuals in the sample could be characterised as differing from one another along the dimensions of cognitive orientation and social interaction. These differences would be expressed as *factor scores:* a combination of the scores on the variables weighted according to their factor loadings.

In terms of our interpretation of the factors as cognitive orientation and social interaction, as there are individual differences in factor scores on the two factors, we could use the scores to define different levels of cognitive orientation and social interaction. "High" and "low" are two obvious levels of cognitive orientation. We could regard those whose factor scores were in the upper 50 per cent of all scores as "high" and the rest as "low" in cognitive orientation. We might then theorise or conjecture that the "high" would perform better on cognitive tasks (such as those involved in academic subjects) than the "low". Hence a relation between scores on the factor and the extent of achievement is being hypothesised. Factors, then, can be regarded as theoretical constructs characterised in terms of qualities such as cognitive orientation and social interaction. Differences in factor scores between people suggest that they differ in the degree to which they possess the hypothetical quality. The relation between these differences and other differences, such as school performance, can then become a subject for research.

The Application of Factor Analysis

Factor analysis has been widely used in the study of personality by R. B. Cattell and H. J. Eysenck. They differ from one another in the data they use, their methods of factor analysis, and the way they regard factors. However, in psychological terms their end-results are very similar in many respects. This might suggest that factor analysis is a rather robust technique which yields a fairly accurate description of personality, despite differences in the methods of analysis and the interpretation of factors between those who use it.

CATTELL

It is a truism in factor analysis that the factors which are obtained are determined by the variables which were originally measured. It would be impossible, therefore, to get a factor of general intelligence out of a factor analysis if intelligence test or item scores were not included in the first place. In recognition of this, the data which Cattell has used in factor analysis have come from a number of sources (Cattell[1]). He refers to the first kind of data as *L*-data. These come from the life record of the individual, and their source is observed everyday behaviour. In practice such data were derived from behaviour ratings by judges to whom the person being rated was well known. A person may be rated by two or three judges on such characteristics as adaptability, conscientiousness, consideration, emotional stability, and so on. Correlations between such ratings are factor analysed, and the resulting factors are labelled in terms of the particular characteristics which load on them.

The second kind of data he calls *Q*-data and these are derived from questionnaire measures of personality characteristics. A major source of difficulty with such data is their susceptibility to faking and distortion. They assume not only that the person has access to the information required by the questions, but also that he has no intentions to fake or distort. It should be noted that *Q*-data are not necessarily limited to questionnaire responses. Cattell considers that information offered in interviews is of a similar type. In spite of their shortcomings Cattell has used these data quite extensively for the assessment of personality. Questionnaires are a relatively easy and quick way of gathering data. In the next chapter we shall consider the ways in which these data may relate to performance in school.

Cattell refers to the third kind of data as *T*-data. These are measurements derived from objective tests, where the behaviour of a subject is observed and measured in a standard situation. Unlike many *Q*-data tests, these tests do not enable the individual to deduce what the interpretation of his test behaviour is likely to be. "Objectivity" in this context therefore refers to this resistance to possible faking or distortion by

TABLE 4.3

Cattell's Source Traits

Data source	Factor	Source trait	Description
L & Q	A	sizothymia vs. affectothymia	reserved, cool vs. outgoing, warm
L & Q	B	intelligence	dull vs. bright
L & Q	C	ego strength	stable, calm vs. emotional, easily upset
L	D	excitability vs. security	nervous, demanding vs. self-control
L & Q	E	submissiveness vs. dominance	humble, conforming vs. assertive, aggressive
L & Q	F	desurgency vs. surgency	sober, prudent vs. enthusiastic, impulsive
L & Q	G	superego strength	expedient, casual vs. conscientious, persevering
L & Q	H	threctia vs. parmia	shy, timid vs. sociable, spontaneous
L & Q	I	harria vs. premsia	tough-minded, realistic vs. tender-minded, sensitive
L	J	coasthenia vs. zeppia	tired, obsessional vs. vigorous, alert
L	K	comention vs. abcultion	refined, cultured vs. philistine, boorish
L & Q	L	alaxia vs. protension	trusting, adaptable vs. suspicious, self-centred
L & Q	M	praxernia vs. autia	practical, careful vs. imaginative, careless
L & Q	N	artlessness vs. shrewdness	forthright, sentimental vs. shrewd, calculating
L & Q	O	guilt proneness	placid, self-assured vs. apprehensiveness, worried
Q	QI	conservatism vs. radicalism	respecting established ideas vs. analytical, free-thinking
Q	Q2	group adherence vs. self-sufficiency	group dependence vs. resourceful independence
Q	Q3	low integration vs. high self-control	low will control vs. controlled self-respect
Q	Q4	ergic tension	relaxed, tranquil vs. tense, frustrated

an individual attempting to meet the tester's requirements. Cattell regards all these data sources as complementary and considers that each can be used in appropriate circumstances for individual assessment. It is implied here that the same factors underlie all three types of data.

Cattell regards the end results of the factor analyses of these data as "source traits" or "functional unities", each factor thereby representing one trait. These traits manifest themselves in behaviour and are considered responsible for that behaviour. They are in that sense to be distinguished from "surface traits", which are correlated personality characteristics having more than one underlying factor. Cattell argues that "introversion-extraversion" is a surface trait which is made up of several underlying source traits. We will consider this further in our subsequent discussion of "second-order" factors.

In Table 4.3, nineteen source traits yielded by factor analysis of *L*- and *Q*-data are shown, together with a brief description of their characteristics. It can been seen that fifteen factors are derived from *L*-data, sixteen from *Q*-data, and that twelve are common to both data sources. The correspondence of all these factors with those derived from *T*-data has not been clearly demonstrated.

When factors are independent of one another they are referred to as *orthogonal* factors. Cattell's factors representing source traits are not independent of one another and are therefore referred to as *oblique* factors. Orthogonal factors are uncorrelated, whereas oblique factors are correlated with one another. Because Cattell's source traits are

TABLE 4.4
Cattell's Second-Order Factors

Factor	Title	Source traits	
I	low vs. high anxiety (*Anxiety*)	L	(protension)
		O	(guilt proneness)
		Q4	(ergic tension)
		C—	(ego weakness)
		H—	(threctia)
		Q3—	(low integration)
II	introversion vs. extraversion (*Extraversion*)	A	(affectothymia)
		E	(dominance)
		F	(surgency)
		H	(parmia)
		Q2—	(group adherence)
III	tender-minded emotionality vs. alert poise (*Alert Poise*)	C	(ego strength)
		E	(dominance)
		F	(surgency)
		N	(shrewdness)
		A—	(sizothymia)
		I—	(harria)
		M—	(praxernia)
IV	subduedness vs. independence (*Independence*)	E	(dominance)
		M	(autia)
		Q1	(radicalism)
		Q2	(self-sufficiency)
		A—	(sizothymia)
		G—	(low superego strength)

correlated it is possible to factor analyse their intercorrelations, and by that means arrive at *second-order* factors. Such factors are regarded by Cattell as representing the "surface traits" to which we referred earlier. Table 4.4 shows the second-order factors which were derived from the Sixteen Personality Factor Questionnaire (16 PF Test) (Cattell and Eber[3]), together with their titles and the source traits which constitute them.

As we shall see in the next chapter many studies have dealt with the relation between performance in school, and the source traits and the second-order factors.

EYSENCK

Eysenck considers that factor analysis of intercorrelations between items or tests alone is unlikely to lead to meaningful factors. He holds that such correlations should be seen in the context of manifest differences between groups, and that they should derive from scientific theorising in psychology (Eysenck[4]). Eysenck's original factor analytic work (Eysenck[5]) used 700 neurotic male soldiers as subjects. Life-history information and ratings by psychiatrists on a large number of traits were subjected to factor analysis. Two factors emerged, which were characterised as introversion-extraversion (*I-E*) and neuroticism (*N*). A large number of subsequent investigations refined these factors, which Eysenck regarded as two basic dimensions along which neurotics and normals differed. Various clinical categories of neurosis were found to be differentially located in the factor space defined by *I-E* and *N*. Figure 4.1 shows the locations of clinically diagnosed neurotic groups in relation to the dimensions of *I-E* and *N*.

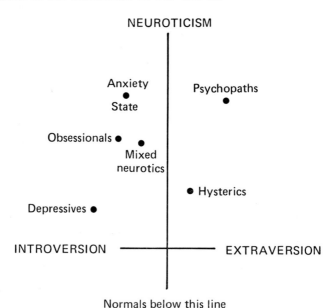

Fig. 4.1 Clinical categories of neurosis in relation to the *N* and *I-E* factors. From Eysenck[6], Fig. 8.

It can be seen that hysterics and psychopaths tend to score on the neuroticism dimension, and the extraversion pole of the *I-E* dimension. On the other hand anxiety neurotics, obsessionals and depressives tend to score on the neuroticism dimension and towards the introversion pole. Normals can be discriminated in terms of their location on the *I-E* dimension.

Eysenck's scheme possesses a very significant biological component which leads him to argue for a hereditary basis for his factors (Eysenck[7]). We can infer from this that the kind of neurosis is determined by the degree of hereditary endowment of *I-E*. The degree of neurosis is held to be largely a function of the hereditary predisposition to neurosis. Both factors, therefore, are regarded by Eysenck as genetically based.

Eysenck[5] regards introverts and extraverts as basic personality types who differ from one another in a large number of personality traits. Eysenck and Eysenck picture the typical extravert and introvert as follows:

> The typical extravert is sociable, likes parties, has many friends, needs to have people to talk to, and does not like reading or studying by himself. He craves excitement, takes chances, often sticks his neck out, acts on the spur of the moment, and is generally an impulsive individual. He is fond of practical jokes, always has a ready answer, and generally likes change; he is carefree, easy-going and likes to "laugh and be merry". He prefers to keep moving and doing things, tends to be aggressive and lose his temper quickly; altogether his feelings are not kept under tight control, and he is not always a reliable person.
>
> The typical introvert is a quiet, retiring sort of person, fond of books rather than people; he is reserved and distant except to intimate friends. He tends to plan ahead, "looks before he leaps", and distrusts the impulse of the moment. He does not like excitement, takes matters of everyday life with proper seriousness, and likes a well-ordered mode of life. He keeps his feelings under close control, seldom behaves in an aggressive manner, and does not lose his temper easily. He is reliable, somewhat pessimistic, and places great value on ethical standards.[8]

Neuroticism is regarded as high emotional reactivity which is mediated by the autonomic nervous system. This autonomic reactivity is characteristic of the neurotic personality type, and according to Eysenck it is genetically based (Eysenck[5]).

Questionnaire measures of *I-E* and *N* have been developed and used extensively in research. The Maudsley Personality Inventory (MPI) (Eysenck[9]) and the Eysenck Personality Inventory (EPI) (Eysenck and Eysenck[10]) have been developed for use with adult populations, and the Junior Eysenck Personality Inventory (JEPI) (Eysenck[11]) can be used with children from the age of seven years. The EPI and the JEPI contain a "lie scale" in order to detect individuals who are faking good responses to the items. Lie scale scores beyond a defined value render the answers to the *I-E* and *N* items unacceptable. As we shall see in a later chapter, these questionnaires have been widely used to study the relation of the *I-E* and *N* personality factors to school performance.

CATTELL AND EYSENCK COMPARED

It can be seen from the previous exposition that Cattell and Eysenck differ in their data sources, their methods of analysis, and their final results in terms of their descriptions of personality. However, perhaps the end results are not as distinct as these differences suggest. Certainly the data sources are different: Eysenck is concerned to distinguish criterion groups in his factor analyses, whereas Cattell's basic concern is to establish source traits.

In the matter of analysis, Cattell prefers oblique solutions on the grounds that these yield a psychologically more meaningful picture. Eysenck uses orthogonal solutions, thus maintaining mathematically independent factors. Cattell's preferences for oblique factors are largely empirical. They lead to easier psychological interpretation and, according to Cattell, are probably truer to nature than are orthogonal factors. Nonetheless, there are issues concerning oblique solutions which should be mentioned. One is that they involve a technique much more difficult to work with, both graphically and computationally. One problem that arises—how oblique the factor axes can be before they should be regarded as one factor—is unanswerable. Correlations among factors could suggest that it is impossible to construct truly independent measures of the factors, an assumption which might be unjustified. On the positive side it could be said that the degree of obliqueness is in itself important information, affecting the interpretation of results. Perhaps the most important point is that since oblique factors are correlated it is possible to factor analyse their intercorrelations and thereby arrive at second-order factors. Cattell's second-order factors I and II (Anxiety and Extraversion) clearly bear a distinctive conceptual relation to Eysenck's *N* and *I-E* factors.

One might say that in the final outcome Cattell and Eysenck are in broad agreement on the interpretation of introversion-extraversion, though they do differ on particular details. Further, their similarities are probably more important than their differences in appreciating the relations of these factors to school attainment. Cattell regards emotional stability as the opposite of Eysenck's neuroticism factor. In this respect anxiety and neuroticism share a great deal of common ground, although in Eysenck's terms neuroticism is not completely characterised by anxiety.

It should be emphasised, however, that these are *similarities of interpretation*. Such similarities do not guarantee that Cattell's and Eysenck's scales do in fact measure similar things. The fact that the art of factorial interpretation in both cases leads to a similar characterisation of some important personality factors does not necessarily mean that the same things have been measured. Nonetheless both approaches have been fruitful in giving us a deeper understanding of the variables which influence school achievement; and the next chapter outlines some findings on the relation between Cattell's source traits and performance in school.

References

[1] R. B. CATTELL, *The Scientific Analysis of Personality*, Penguin, Harmondsworth, 1965.

[2] R. B. CATTELL, A. P. SEALEY and A. B. SWENEY, "What Can Personality and Motivation Source Trait Measurements add to the Prediction of School Achievement?", *British Journal of Educational Psychology*, 1966, **36**, pp. 280-95.

[3] R. B. CATTELL and H. W. EBER, *Manual for Forms A and B Sixteen Personality Factor Questionnaire*, Institute for Personality and Ability Testing, Champaign, 1962.

[4] H. J. EYSENCK, *The Structure of Human Personality*, Routledge and Kegan Paul, London, 1953.

[5] H. J. EYSENCK, *Dimensions of Personality*, Routledge and Kegan Paul, London, 1947.

[6] H. J. EYSENCK, *The Dynamics of Anxiety and Hysteria*, Routledge and Kegan Paul, London, 1957.

[7] H. J. EYSENCK, *The Biological Basis of Personality*, Charles C. Thomas, Springfield, 1967.

[8] S. B. G. EYSENCK and H. J. EYSENCK, "The Validity of Questionnaires and Rating Assessments of Extraversion and Neuroticism and their Factorial Validity", *British Journal of Psychology*, 1963, **54**, pp. 51-62.

[9] H. J. EYSENCK, *Manual of the Maudsley Personality Inventory*, University of London Press, London, 1959.

[10] H. J. EYSENCK and S. B. G. EYSENCK, *Manual of the Eysenck Personality Inventory*, University of London Press, London, 1964.

[11] S. B. G. EYSENCK, *Manual of the Junior Eysenck Personality Inventory*, University of London Press, London, 1965.

Chapter 5

Source Traits and
School Attainment

Personality questionnaries which purport to measure the source traits derived from Q-data (Cattell[1]) have been developed for a number of age groups. The 16 PF test measures sixteen of the source traits or personality factors in adults (Cattell and Eber[2]). The High School Personality Questionnaire (HSPQ) measures fourteen primary and two second-order factors among high school pupils (Cattell and Cattell[3]). The Children's Personality Questionnaire (CPQ) provides measures on fourteen personality factors among younger children (Porter, Cattell and Ford[4]). The factors are held to be comparable at the three levels.

Some studies have related these factors to school attainment in an attempt to find which factors above and beyond sheer cognitive ability reliably relate to performance. Butcher, Ainsworth and Nesbitt[5] (Part II, Chapter 14) set out to compare the personalities of British and American schoolchildren, and to establish the relation between personality factors and school achievement. The HSPQ was administered to all the seventh-grade children in an urban and a rural school in Illinois. The criteria of achievement for these American children were (1) the Stanford Intermediate Achievement Test (Form K), which yields six subscores for paragraph meaning, word meaning, spelling, language, arithmetic reasoning and arithmetic computation, together with a total score; and (2) teacher ratings of children's behaviour on a seven-point scale.

Two British samples were used. The first consisted of all first-year children in a secondary modern school in Manchester; the second consisted of 140 children in the third year of secondary school who were representative of their age group in ability and socio-economic status. In this way the investigators were able to compare national as well as international differences. The criterion of achievement for the British children was their performance in the annual examinations in English, Mathematics, History, Geography, Science and Art.

The comparison of the personalities of the American rural and urban children is shown in Table 5.1.

TABLE 5.1

**Significant Mean Differences between American
Urban and Rural Children ***

Trait	Factor	Urban mean	Rural mean	Difference	t	Significance of difference
Ego strength	C	8·92	10·47	1·55	4·74	0·0001
Adventurousness	H	8·39	9·56	1·17	3·56	0·001
Passive individualism	J	10·68	9·86	0·82	3·06	0·01
Timidity	O	10·68	9·42	1·26	3·64	0·001
Tenseness	Q4	9·32	8·68	0·64	1·99	0·05
Extraversion		69·81	73·86	4·05	3·12	0·01
Anxiety		109·47	101·74	7·73	3·76	0·001
		(N = 154)	(N = 123)			

* Adapted from Butcher, H. J. et al[5]. Table 1.

The rural children were found to be significantly higher on factors C (ego strength) and H (adventurousness). They were significantly lower on factors J (passive individualism), O (timidity) and Q4 (tenseness). On the second-order factors the rural children were significantly more extraverted and less anxious than the city children.

The American children differed from the British Secondary Modern children on nine of the fourteen primary factors. These differences are shown in Table 5.2.

TABLE 5.2

**Significant Mean Differences between American and
British Secondary Modern Children ***

Trait	Factor	American mean	British mean	Difference	t	Significance of difference
Sociability	A	11·32	9·77	1·55	6·17	0·0001
Intelligence	B	13·92	11·92	2·00	8·85	0·0001
Ego Strength	C	9·58	9·07	0·51	2·10	0·05
Excitability	D	9·48	10·12	0·64	2·78	0·01
Assertion	E	9·08	11·13	2·05	8·51	0·0001
Conscientiousness	G	12·34	10·63	1·71	6·55	0·0001
Timidity	O	10·09	11·24	1·15	4·58	0·0001
Self-Control	Q3	10·38	9·68	0·70	3·20	0·01
Tenseness	Q4	9·04	10·24	1·20	5·26	0·0001
Extraversion		71·61	68·14	3·47	3·48	0·001
Anxiety		105·98	114·24	8·26	5·91	0·0001
		(N = 277)	(N = 230)			

* Adapted from Butcher, H. J. et al[5]. Table 2.

The American children were significantly more sociable (factor A), were more intelligent (factor B), possessed more ego strength (factor C), were more conscientious (factor G) and more self-controlled (factor Q3). They were significantly less excitable (factor D), less dominant and assertive (factor E), and less timid (factor O). Their level of tenseness was also significantly lower than that of the British children. The American children were significantly more extraverted and less anxious than the British children.

It should be borne in mind that many of these differences were probably due to the special nature of the British sample. Secondary Modern school children are those who were not selected for Grammar school. The American sample was unselected in this respect, and therefore significant differences in intelligence were to be expected. Other evidence indicates that lower-stream children tend to be more anxious than upper-stream children (Cox[6], Cox and Hammond[7], Levy, Gooch and Kellmer-Pringle[8]), which accords with the differences found here by Butcher, Ainsworth and Nesbitt[5].

It is not surprising that many of these differences disappeared when the American children were compared with the representative sample of British children. Table 5.3 shows these comparisons.

TABLE 5.3
Significant Mean Differences between American and British Children *

Trait	Factor	American mean	British mean	Difference	t	Significance of difference
Sociability	A	5·22	4·74	0·48	2·61	0·01
Assertion	E	4·76	5·66	0·90	5·11	0·0001
Conscientiousness	G	6·13	5·19	0·94	5·84	0·0001
Sensitivity	I	4·52	4·01	0·51	2·55	0·05
		(N = 277)	(N = 140)			

* Adapted from Butcher, H. J. et al[5]. Table 3.

The Americans were still more sociable and conscientious than the British, and, in this case, they were also significantly more sensitive (factor I). However, the remaining differences which appeared in the comparison with British Secondary Modern children were not maintained with the representative sample.

The relation between the personality factors and school performance was predictably rather complicated. Table 5.4 shows some of the

TABLE 5.4
Significant Correlations Between Some Personality Factors and Achievement in the American Samples *

SIAT Subtest	Sociability A		Conscientiousness G		Self-sufficiency Q2	
	American urban	American rural	American urban	American rural	American urban	American rural
Total	0·17		0·34	0·18	0·35	
Paragraph meaning		0·19	0·32	0·17	0·35	0·19
Word meaning			0·29	0·21	0·32	0·19
Spelling	0·25		0·33	0·23	0·18	
Language	0·21		0·34		0·22	
Arithmetic meaning	0·19		0·31		0·35	
Arithmetic computation	0·19		0·36	0·22	0·26	
Teacher rating on behaviour			0·18			

* Adapted from Butcher, H. J. et al[5]. Tables 4 and 5.

significant relationships. With the exception of intelligence (factor B), the correlations of the personality factors and performance were of a low order. Nonetheless there were some interesting general trends. Conscientiousness (factor G) and self-sufficiency (factor Q2) showed significant correlations with performance in all samples, in that the more conscientious and self-sufficient tended to perform better. The criteria of achievement were different between samples: the American criteria were the scores on the six subtests of the Stanford Intermediate Achievement Test, whereas the British criterion was performance in annual examinations. The factors tended to predict over the whole range of these criteria. Sociability (factor A) correlated significantly with performance in the American sample, but not so in the British samples. Table 5.5 shows the relation of G and Q2 to performance in the

TABLE 5.5

Significant Correlations Between Some Personality Factors and Achievement in the British Secondary Modern Sample *

Subject	Personality factor	
	Conscientiousness G	Self-sufficiency Q2
English	0·15	0·13
Maths		0·15
Science		0·14
History		0·14
Geography		0·16
Art	0·22	

* Adapted from Butcher, H. J. et al[5]. Table 6.

British Secondary Modern sample. Butcher, Ainsworth and Nesbitt[5] suggested that this may represent a genuine cultural difference. Certainly if the cultural conditions for sociability differ between the United States and Britain, it is possible that the items which were appropriate to factor A in the United States would be inappropriate in a British setting.

The proportion of variance in achievement predicted by particular personality factors was quite low, and did not exceed 13 per cent except in the case of intelligence (factor B). Further, it is not clear whether this percentage is in addition to or beyond the proportion which intelligence itself predicts.

A later study by Cattell, Sealy and Sweney[9] showed the relation between both G and Q3 (conscientiousness and self-sentiment) and school performance to be significant and positive. These findings seem to be well within the bounds of expectations based on common sense. In broader terms their paper reported results on the percentage of achievement variance which can be predicted from personality and motivational source traits. Table 5.6 summarises some of these results. Their findings suggested that, using these measures, up to 200 per cent more variance could be predicted from these combinations than from intelligence alone. However, it should be noted that in their study they had a large number of variables and relatively small samples of

TABLE 5.6

Multiple Prediction of Achievement from Various Combinations of Intelligence, Personality and Motivational Traits ($N = 144$) *

Measure	No. of variables	Standard Achievement Test			
		Multiple R	Corrected for shrinkage	% of achievement variance predicted	
				uncorrected	corrected
Intelligence	I	0·50		25	—
Intelligence + HSPQ Personality Factors (excluding Intelligence)	14	0·79	0·73	62	53
Intelligence + HSPQ Factors (excluding Intelligence) + Motivational Traits	32	0·85	0·73	72	53

* Adapted from Cattell, R. B. et al[9]. Table 10, p. 291.

school children, and as a result there are good technical reasons for doubting the reliability of the results. These reasons arise from the methods by which multiple correlations are computed. The product moment correlation between two variables has been constantly referred to throughout this book. Multiple correlation (R) refers to the correlation among three or more variables. Its method of calculation tends to capitalise on chance deviations in a way which favours an inflated value of R. Obtained values of R therefore have to be corrected for "shrinkage", which would occur in a new sample where different chance deviations would be operating. The corrections for shrinkage which Cattell et al.[9] carried out suggested that on a new sample the amount of variance in performance accounted for by intelligence plus personality traits plus motivation could "shrink" by as much as fifty per cent. Whether, therefore, the authors have increased predictive power by 200 per cent remains yet to be seen. A further analysis on 278 children revealed that 52 per cent of the variance in classroom grades was predicted by the three measures combined. In this case the increase was just over 100 per cent. It also accorded with what would be predicted from the Rs corrected for shrinkage (Table 5.6). Further studies with much larger samples are needed so that the reliability of these results can be assessed.

A study by Rushton[10] (Part II, Chapter 15) using CPQ measures of the source traits, found patterns relating trait measures and the cognitive abilities measured by the "Eleven-plus" examination in England for 458 ten- and eleven-year-old boys and girls. In some respects the patterns were similar to those found by Butcher et al.[5] in their study with older children. Table 5.7 summarises the relationships. Factors C (ego strength) G (conscientiousness) and F (enthusiasm) had positive correlations with attainment. The second-order factors of anxiety and neuroticism were negatively correlated with cognitive

TABLE 5.7

Significant Correlations Between Some Personality Factors and Performance on the Eleven-plus Examination *

Trait	Factor	Verbal reasoning	Arithmetic	English	Spatial	School record	Pass vs. fail
Ego strength	C	0·15	0·14	0·15	0·12	0·20	−0·22
Enthusiasm	F	0·15	0·12	0·16		0·11	−0·14
Conscientiousness	G	0·18	0·16	0·14		0·18	−0·13
Anxiety		−0·20	−0·15	−0·16	−0·10	−0·20	0·15
Extraversion		0·16	0·11	0·13		0·15	−0·14

* Adapted from Rushton[10], Table I.

ability and school performance, whereas the second-order factor of extraversion correlated positively with performance. Those findings go beyond those of Butcher et al.[5] to suggest that, at least in this age level, stable extraverted boys and girls gain some advantage over the others in performance.

The results of both studies do not support detailed generalisations. Although many significant correlations were reported they tended to be of a low order. The amount of variance in the performance criteria accounted for by particular factors therefore tended to be low, and in Rushton's study never exceeded 5 per cent. Overall the results tended to be indicative rather than conclusive, suggesting points of departure for further work rather than providing the final word on the matter.

Butcher et al.[5] pointed out that the HSPQ might lack the precision necessary for the purpose of predicting school attainment. Since each factor is only measured by ten items, the factor scores are much more likely to be affected by random error. However, in so far as some factors are consistently correlated with performance, such as G and Q2 in Butcher et al.[5] and factor C in Rushton[10], it would seem promising to increase the number of items which index these factors, with the specific aim of predicting school performance.

In general the trends were such that among ten- and eleven-year-olds, low-anxious non-neurotic extraverts tended to perform better in school. The reasons for this are unclear, but some theroretical considerations which bear on this will be discussed in the next chapter. Among early secondary schoolchildren there were personality differences between urban and rural children and between British and American children. Even with these differences, however, there are some factors, particularly conscientiousness and self-sufficient resourcefulness, which are consistently correlated positively with performance. Much more work is needed, however, both in the development of measures and the replication of the studies, so that the full reliability and significance of these results can be established.

References

[1] R. B. CATTELL, *The Scientific Analysis of Personality*, Penguin, Harmondsworth, 1965.

[2] R. B. CATTELL and H. W. EBER, *Manual for Forms A and B Sixteen Personality Factor Questionnaire*, Institute for Personality and Ability Testing, Champaign, 1962.

[3] R. B. CATTELL and M. D. L. CATTELL, *Handbook for the Jr.-Sr. High School Personality Questionnaire*, Institute for Personality and Ability Testing, Champaign, 1969.

[4] R. B. PORTER, R. B. CATTELL and J. J. FORD, *Manual for the Children's Personality Questionnaire "CPQ"*, Institute for Personality and Ability Testing, Champaign, 1968.

[5] H. J. BUTCHER, M. AINSWORTH and J. E. NESBITT, "Personality Factors and School Achievement, a Comparison of British and American Children", *British Journal of Educational Psychology*, 1963, **33**, pp. 276-86.

[6] F. N. COX, "Educational Streaming and General and Test Anxiety", *Child Development*, 1962, **33**, pp. 381-90.

[7] F. N. COX and S. B. HAMMOND, "Educational Streaming and Anxiety in Children", *Australian Journal of Education*, 1964, **8**, pp. 85-90.

[8] P. LEVY, S. GOOCH and M. L. KELLMER-PRINGLE, "A Longitudinal Study of the Relationship between Anxiety and Streaming in a Progressive and a Traditional Junior School", *British Journal of Educational Psychology*, 1969, **39**, pp. 166-73.

[9] R. B. CATTELL, A. P. SEALEY and A. B. SWENEY, "What can Personality and Motivation Source Trait Measurements Add to the Prediction of School Achievement?", *British Journal of Educational Psychology*, 1966, **36**, pp. 280-95.

[10] J. RUSHTON, "The Relationship between Personality Characteristics and Scholastic Success in Eleven-Year-Old Children", *British Journal of Educational Psychology*, 1966, **36**, pp. 178-84.

Chapter 6

Neuroticism, Introversion-Extraversion and Attainment

In the preceding chapter a series of studies was reported concerning the relation of Cattell's source and surface traits of personality to school performance. The findings suggested that, at least among primary school children, stable extraverts tended to be the better performers. A considerable amount of research on the relation between academic performance and Eysenck's factors of Neuroticism and Introversion-Extraversion has been reported in the last decade. This relation tended to change according to the level of education which was used as the criterion of performance.

Eysenck[1] put forward a theoretical account of the differing performance characteristics of introverts and extraverts. In Chapter 4 the qualities of the introvert and the extravert were described briefly by Eysenck and Eysenck[2]. It will be recalled that the extravert tended to be sociable, impulsive, aggressive and lacking in reliability; whereas the introvert tended to be retiring, bookish, well-organised and controlled. This suggests that, in an educational context, introverts should be better learners than extraverts. Eysenck's theory implied that, in laboratory studies of conditionability, introverts should be more quickly conditioned than extraverts, and that the introvert's conditioned responses should decay more slowly. Franks[3] found that the predicted relation between conditionability and *I-E* as measured by the Maudsley Personality Inventory (MPI) (Eysenck[4]) was significant. These findings were therefore in accordance with Eysenck's theory.

Spence[5] presented evidence that conditionability in humans was related to high drive. Scores on anxiety scales have been held to reflect the level of emotionally based drive (Taylor,[6] Jensen,[7] Lynn and Gordon,[8] Gaudry and Spielberger[9]). Since anxiety and neuroticism are highly associated, scores on Eysenck's Neuroticism factor have also been regarded as a drive index (Eysenck,[1] Lynn[10]). The relation between drive and performance is expressed by the Yerkes-Dodson law, which holds that high drive tends to facilitate performance on easier tasks, but to interfere with performance on more difficult tasks. Gaudry and Spielberger[9] have shown that the effects of anxiety on educational achievement cannot be considered separately from the effects of intellectual ability, in that some evidence indicates that high-anxious students of high ability tend to perform better than low-anxious students of high ability. To the extent that neuroticism is an index of drive, we might expect similar results from a study of the relation between *N* and academic performance.

Furneaux[11] and Broadbent[12] showed that high attainers among university students were significantly more neurotic and introverted than low attainers. These results are congruent with inferences from the theory of Eysenck[1]. However they do provide an interesting contrast with the findings of Rushton,[13] which were referred to in the previous chapter. There, among ten- and eleven-year-old children, stable extraverts tended to be the higher performers. This suggests that, in an educational context, the relation between attainment and the *I-E* and *N* factors may be more complex than Eysenck's theory indicates.

Some Empirical Studies

Using Eysenck's theory as a point of departure, Lynn[14] (Part II, Chapter 16) compared the scores on the MPI of university students and non-university controls. Table 6.1 shows his results.

TABLE 6.I

Mean *N* and *E* Scores on the MPI for the Norming Samples, the Control Samples and the University Student Samples *

Group		Norms	Controls	Students
Men	No.	200	100	115
	Neuroticism	17·8	21·2	25·5
	Extraversion	24·6	29·3	22·4
Women	No.	200	67	96
	Neuroticism	19·4	23·8	28·2
	Extraversion	25·2	28·5	22·9

* Adapted from Lynn[14], Table I.

The students were significantly more neurotic and introverted than were the control group. The findings mentioned in the previous chapter indicated that Cattell's second-order anxiety factor was negatively correlated with attainment in school, as was his second-order neuroticism factor (Rushton[13]). Implicit in Lynn's work, however, is a positive correlation between neuroticism and attendance at university. Since Lynn presents no data on the *performance* of neurotic university students, we cannot draw from his results alone any inference concerning performance differences between high- and low-neurotic university students. It may be that the university provides a stressful environment which produces neuroticism in students; and that in turn this neuroticism causes students to fail or drop out. All Lynn's students were in fact in first year university. His predictions could have further implications if his results were maintained through all years.

Savage[15] (Part II, Chapter 17) suggested that even though university students might show a higher incidence of neuroticism than the general community, it was possible that excessively high neuroticism might be detrimental to academic success. The MPI was given to 168 Arts students during their second term, and their N and I-E scores were related to the results obtained in their annual examinations. Table 6.2 shows the mean N and I-E scores in relation to the number of subjects passed. Both scores were shown to be significantly related to performance. Savage argued that students who passed two subjects or less

TABLE 6.2
Mean N and E Scores in Relation to Number of Subjects Passed *

Factor	Subjects passed				
	0	1	2	3	4
Neuroticism	40·0	31·2	27·1	28·1	26·2
Extraversion	36·2	35·1	28·2	25·5	26·1

* Adapted from Savage[15].

out of four possessed significantly higher N scores than the rest, even though the means on N for all levels of performance were significantly beyond that for the general community. This led Savage to suggest the possibility that there was an optimum level of N which was facilitating in performance, beyond which performance was impaired. In terms of the results which Savage has presented (Table 6.2) we must be careful not to take this argument too literally. The results show that students who failed three or four subjects were much more neurotic than the rest, who appear to be comparable in their Neuroticism scores. Also, his argument for a U-shaped relationship between neuroticism and academic achievement is highly speculative when his results are considered. It is true that the mean N scores for all his groups were greater than the mean of the norming sample of the MPI. However, it cannot be concluded from this that a middle level of neuroticism has facilitated performance. If the argument were to be one of substance, it would need to be shown that stable students were in fact impaired in performance. Savage's "suggested" U-shaped relationship is not, therefore, the sole suggestion which might be made. The linear nature of his own results could also suggest that stable students might perform very well. The findings for I-E were in accordance with those of Furneaux and Lynn, suggesting therefore the further possibility that there were interactions between N and I-E in determining a level of performance.

In a further study Savage[16] correlated scores on an intelligence test with performance on the Junior Eysenck Personality Inventory (JEPI) (Eysenck[17]) and scores on standardised tests of reading and arithmetic, in a sample of junior school children. The JEPI measures the I-E and N factors and incorporates a lie scale. Significant positive correlations were found between IQ and extraversion ($0·27$), and between extraversion and arithmetic score ($0·24$). The correlation between extraversion and reading score was positive ($0·19$) but failed to reach significance. A significant negative correlation was reported between N and reading score (-0.22), which suggests that the more neurotic children tended to be poorer readers. These results are in contrast with those found in university students, but are in line with those of Rushton.[13]

Lynn and Gordon[8] had suggested that neuroticism would impair learning on difficult tasks but facilitate the learning of simple tasks. This is an application of the Yerkes-Dodson law, which states that the optimum drive required for efficient learning is inversely related to task difficulty. In a study of the operation of this law in learning in rats, Broadhurst[18] showed that in a task of moderate complexity, high and low emotionality were less effective than moderate emotionality in facilitating learning. Accordingly, Lynn and Gordon predicted that the performance of 60 university students on Raven's Progressive Matrices (a non-verbal intelligence test judged to be of moderate complexity for university students) would be affected by neuroticism in accordance with the Yerkes-Dodson law. Thus high and low N scorers on the MPI would perform poorly on the matrices compared with the middle N scorers. This prediction was confirmed in their results. Table 6.3 shows the curvilinear relation between the level of neuroticism and the mean scores on the progressive matrices.

TABLE 6.3
Mean Progressive Matrices Scores for Six Levels of N *

N level	Mean score on progressive matrices[a]
1 (high)	23
2	23
3	24
4	25
5	23
6 (low)	22

* Adapted from Lynn and Gordon[8], Fig. I.
[a] These means are expressed to the nearest whole number.

This curvilinear relation demonstrates an inadequacy in correlational studies of the relation between personality variables and school attainment. Such studies assume that the relation between the variables being studied is linear. Low values of correlation might therefore be produced by non-linear relations between the variables.

Entwistle and Cunningham[19] (Part II, Chapter 18) investigated further the relation between N, I-E and attainment. The data used in their study came from a longitudinal study of 3286 Aberdeen school children. Two analyses of the data were performed: (1) a correlational analysis of the relations among variables, and (2) a regression analysis to establish whether the relation of attainment to N and I-E was linear. Of the total sample, 2707 children had completed verbal and non-verbal reasoning tests, English and arithmetic attainment tests, and the JEPI, and were rank ordered by teachers on attainment in secondary school subjects. Correlations of all the variables with scores on the N factor of

TABLE 6.4

**Correlation of Attainment and Reasoning Scores
with N and I-E at Various Ages** (N=2707) *

Test	Age	N	I-E
Teachers' estimate	13	—0·16	0·02
Verbal reasoning	13	—0·14	0·05
Teachers' estimate	12	—0·14	0·04
Verbal reasoning	12	—0·13	0·05
Non-verbal reasoning	11	—0·12	0·06

*Adapted from Entwistle and Cunningham[19], Tables 3 and 4.

the JEPI were negative (Table 6.4), and the regression analysis showed that the relation of attainment to Neuroticism was linear (Fig. 6.1).

The low values of correlation between *I-E* and attainment (Table 6.4) was accounted for by the non-linearity of that relation. As Fig. 6.2 reveals, the relationship was U-shaped. However, the contribution of

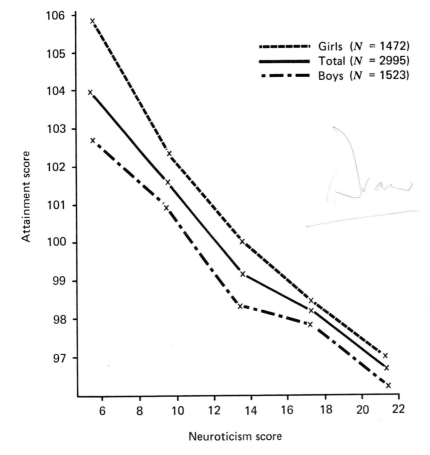

Fig. 6.1 Regression lines for attainment score on neuroticism. From Entwistle and Cunningham[19], p. 127.

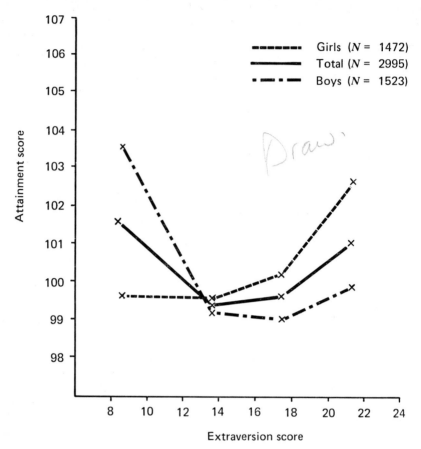

Fig. 6.2 Regression lines for attainment score on extraversion. From Entwistle and Cunningham[19], p. 128.

the sexes to this composite was quite different: extraverted girls and introverted boys were the highest attainers. In both sexes stability also contributed to high attainment. Importantly, none of the results indicated that neurotic introverts were superior in school work.

The results to this point suggested that stability and extraversion in school children were associated with high achievement; whereas in university students high achievement was associated with neuroticism and introversion. The findings of Entwistle and Cunningham indicated that sex differences were an important consideration in accounting for the relation of personality variables to performance. There were also other very significant differences between young school children and university students: school children represent the whole range of ability and attainment, whereas in both these respects university students are highly selected. Simple statistical treatments of data of the correlational kind obscure the complexities introduced by curvilinear relations, and could mask possible interactions between variables in determining outcomes. It is also of interest that the school children's results appear to represent a departure from Eysenck's theory; but this may be only because the difficulty level of school subjects for a particular child is hard to determine. Eysenck and Cookson[20] suggested that the introvert might be a "late developer" in relation to performance. Their results indicated that there was no sex difference in the advantage which extraverts showed in performance. However, their investigation used a sample of eleven-year-old children. Entwistle and Cunningham's sample comprised thirteen-year-olds, and Eysenck and Cookson suggested that those results reflected the possibility that the introverted boys were earlier "late developers" than the introverted girls. However the differences might be accounted for, it is beyond dispute that different investigations have yielded different results. As Eysenck and Cookson point out, the complexity of the results certainly indicates a need for further and better experimentation and theorising.

Further complications are introduced by Entwistle and Welsh[21]. They correlated scores on the JEPI with attainment for groups of high- and low-ability boys and girls. Over the whole range of ability the sex difference in the relation of *I-E* to school performance was similar to that reported in Entwistle and Cunningham[19], that is, introverted boys and extraverted girls tended to perform better in class. However, high-ability introverts and low-ability extraverts among boys performed better than their classmates of equal ability but of the opposite personality type. Among girls, low-ability extraverts tended to perform better than the introverts, but at the high-ability level no significant differences in performance emerged. Therefore not only were there sex differences in the relation of *I-E* to performance, but also differences within the sexes between high- and low-ability groups.

The possible explanations of these differences are at best speculative. Entwistle and Cunningham[19] suggested that there might be sex differences in peer group influences between introverts and extraverts which influenced performance. In addition, it is possible that the personality characteristics which are appropriate to academic development in one kind of educational setting are inappropriate in another. Interactions between personality characteristics and the demands of particular educational settings await detailed investigation.

A study by Finlayson[22] (Part II, Chapter 19) showed changes in the relationship between a JEPI measure of *N* and *I-E* and performance over a three-year period. His subjects were all Grammar School boys, and their scores on the standardised English (EQ) and Arithmetic (AQ) tests in the "Eleven-plus" examination reflect their high ability. The boys were divided into four groups of high- and low-neurotic introverts and extraverts according to their scores on the JEPI. There were 32 boys in each group. The results indicate that there were no significant differences between introverts and extraverts, and high and low neurotics, in the scores derived from the "Eleven-plus" examination. At the end of the first year at Grammar School, some differences in performance (as measured by a composite score in English, mathematics, science and a foreign language) began to emerge. There were no statistically significant differences in performance, but the mean scores for the first year examination distinctly favoured the introverts.

TABLE 6.5

Mean Examination Scores for the E and I Groups over Three Years *

Personality	Ist year	2nd year	3rd year
Extraversion	189·36	187·55	181·14
Introversion	209·71	219·36	233·36

* Adapted from Finlayson[22], Table 2.

Table 6.5 summarises Finlayson's results for the extraverts and introverts over the three-year period. It shows that there was a progressive decline in the extraverts' performance and a progressive improvement in the introverts' performance over the time period. In the second and third years, the differences in performance between the introverts and extraverts were statistically significant. This is in accordance with the finding of Entwistle and Welsh[21] that introverted boys of high ability tended to be higher attainers than extraverted boys.

Also, the relation of neuroticism to attainment became more manifest with each year of education. The differences between high and low neurotics in examination performance in first and second year was not statistically significant, but the mean values did favour the low neurotics.

TABLE 6.6

**Mean Examination Scores for the High and Low N Groups
over Three Years** *

Neuroticism	Ist year	2nd year	3rd year
Low	205·55	213·49	213·19
High	193·52	193·41	191·31

* Adapted from Finlayson[22], Table 2.

Table 6.6 shows the performance trend over the three years for the low- and high-neurotic boys. The difference in third year was statistically significant, and the second year difference closely approached significance. An interesting relation between *I-E* and high neuroticism also emerged. The performance of high-neurotic extraverts declined significantly over the three-year period, while there was a non-significant improvement in the performance of high-neurotic introverts. This trend is congruent with the higher degree of neuroticism and introversion among university students (Furneaux,[11] Lynn[14]).

It should be noted that the statistical analysis which Finlayson employed has a distinct advantage: it does not assume that the relations among variables are linear, and therefore the trends in the data are more readily discerned. However, the study does make the assumption that *I-E* and *N* are stable qualities of the pupils over the time period, from only one measurement on the JEPI at the beginning of their second year in school. The assumption of stability in these qualities might be begging a very important empirical question. It may be that the changes in performances over the three-year period were due to changes in personality characteristics. The hypothesis of a genetic base for such factors connotes stability over time, but we have no reason to treat that hypothesis as a fact.

Altogether the studies show that the relations between *N*, *I-E* and academic performance change over time. In primary school it seems clear that stable extraversion had the strongest relation to school performance, and neurotic introverts were disadvantaged (Rushton;[13] Savage[16]). In secondary school the relations were more complex and apparently sex-linked (Entwistle and Cunningham;[19] Eysenck and Cookson[20]). Introverted boys and extraverted girls were favoured in attainment, which led Eysenck and Cookson to suggest that introverts may be "late developers," and that introverted boys develop more quickly than introverted girls. In the results of Finlayson,[22] introversion increasingly favoured the performance of boys in Grammar School, as did stability. However, among neurotic boys the performance of extraverts tended to deteriorate over time. In the university, introverts seemed to be favoured in attainment, but the influence of neuroticism was not clear. As a group, university students showed higher mean *N* scores on the MPI than the general community, but the pattern of the relation between neuroticism and performance remained unclear. The results of Savage[15] suggested that the relation between *N* and performance might be curvilinear, since in his study the performance of extreme neurotics was impaired. However, without reliable data on the performance of stable students this remains no more than a suggestion.

In the light of the evidence which has been reviewed, it seems beyond question that the relation of *N* and *I-E* to academic attainment changes as education progresses. The cause of these changes is unclear. No one would dispute that primary schools and universities provide very different learning environments for the individual, and these can be presumed to have very different effects on the ways in which knowledge is acquired. A very important question here is whether the stable, extraverted school child becomes the neurotic, introverted university student. Eysenck's theory of personality types whose genesis is constitutional suggests that *I-E* and *N* are relatively fixed properties of the individual. On this basis it does not seem possible to infer the profound changes in personality which the empirical results would require. If, on the other hand, there is good reason to believe that pupils who start out as high or low attainers tend to continue as such, then one can infer that their personality characteristics do change. This issue requires a careful longitudinal study for it to be resolved. Profound changes in personality would not support the genetic hypothesis. Cross-sectional studies of the relationship between personality factors and attainment can yield no index of personality change. A longitudinal study is the most appropriate way to observe changes in personality and attainment, and the relation between them.

References

[1] H. J. EYSENCK, *The Dynamics of Anxiety and Hysteria*, Routledge and Kegan Paul, London, 1957.

[2] S. B. G. EYSENCK and H. J. EYSENCK, "The Validity of Questionnaires and Rating Assessments of Extraversion and Neuroticism and their Factorial Validity", *British Journal of Psychology*, 1963, **54**, pp. 51-62.

[3] C. M. FRANKS, "Personality Factors and the Rate of Conditioning", *British Journal of Psychology*, 1957, **48**, pp. 119-26.

[4] H. J. EYSENCK, *Manual of the Maudsley Personality Inventory*, University of London Press, London, 1959.

[5] K. W. SPENCE, "A Theory of Emotionally Based Drive (*D*) and its Relation to Performance in Simple Learning Situations", *American Psychologist*, 1958, **13**, pp. 131-41.

[6] J. A. TAYLOR, "Drive Theory and Manifest Anxiety", *Psychological Bulletin*, 1956, **53**, pp. 303-20.

[7] A. R. JENSEN, "Personality", *Annual Review of Psychology*, 1958, **9**, pp. 295-322.

[8] R. LYNN and I. E. GORDON, "The Relation of Neuroticism and Extraversion to Intelligence and Educational Attainment", *British Journal of Educational Psychology*, 1961, **31**, pp. 194-203.

[9] E. GAUDRY and C. D. SPIELBERGER, *Anxiety and Educational Achievement*, John Wiley & Sons, Sydney, 1971.

[10] R. LYNN, *An Introduction to the Study of Personality*, Macmillan, London, 1971.

[11] W. D. FURNEAUX, "Some Psychometric Characteristics of University Students Seeking Psychiatric Help", *Bulletin of the British Psychological Society*, 1956, **29**, p. 7.

[12] D. E. BROADBENT, *Perception and Communication*, Permagon Press, London, 1958.

[13] J. RUSHTON, "The Relationship between Personality Characteristics and Scholastic Success in Eleven-Year-Old Children", *British Journal of Educational Psychology*, 1966, **36**, pp. 178-84.

[14] R. LYNN, "Two Personality Characteristics Related to Academic Achievement", *British Journal of Educational Psychology*, 1959, **29**, pp. 213-16.

[15] R. D. SAVAGE, "Personality Factors and Academic Performance", *British Journal of Educational Psychology*, 1962, **32**, pp. 251-53.

[16] R. D. SAVAGE, "Personality Factors and Academic Attainment in Junior School Children", *British Journal of Educational Psychology*, 1966, **36**, pp. 91-92.

[17] S. B. G. EYSENCK, *Manual of the Junior Eysenck Personality Inventory*, University of London Press, London, 1965.

[18] P. BROADHURST, "Emotionality and the Yerkes-Dodson Law", *Journal of Experimental Psychology*, 1957, **54**, pp. 345-52.

[19] N. J. ENTWISTLE and S. CUNNINGHAM, "Neuroticism and School Attainment—A Linear Relationship?", *British Journal of Educational Psychology*, 1968, **38**, pp. 123-32.

[20] H. J. EYSENCK and D. COOKSON, "Personality in Primary School Children: 1. Ability and Achievement", *British Journal of Educational Psychology*, 1969, **39**, pp. 109-30.

[21] N. J. ENTWISTLE and J. WELSH, "Correlates of School Attainment at Different Ability Levels", *British Journal of Educational Psychology*, 1969, **39**, pp. 57-63.

[22] D. S. FINLAYSON, "A Follow-up Study of School Achievement in Relation to Personality", *British Journal of Educational Psychology*, 1970, **40**, pp. 344-49.

Chapter 7

Personality and Attainment: Summary and Prospects

The principal task of this book has been to examine some of the research evidence concerning the relation between personality and school achievement. Its source has been the empirical research which bears on this issue rather than the various theories of personality. The reason for this was that the implications of many theories of personality for educational practice are obscure; the apparent plausibility of most theories is not sufficient reason to force educational practices into their framework. We have not attempted to divine that optimal set of educational circumstances which creates the conditions for personal "growth". Nor have we been concerned with educational "efficiency" thereby assuming the existence of an inevitable end-point for learning experiences defining an "education". These speculative or philosophical endeavours may be quite valid provided that they do not make assumptions which involve the begging of empirical questions. Hence the concern here has been to take those aspects of education and personality which have been subjected to measurement, to see if consistent, orderly and systematic relations are present between personality characteristics and attainment.

This has meant that nearly all the studies which have been considered are implicitly or explicitly correlational in design. To that extent they are descriptive studies pointing to the relational features of personality characteristics and achievement, rather than establishing causal sequences in those relations. An explanation, however, presupposes a situation to be explained; and it is necessary to establish the nature of such situations as the preamble to theorising and experiment.

Our review has shown that the situations to be explained are multiple and complex. And in spite of the foregoing formal caveat concerning explanation it is important to recognise that even the discovery of empirical relations is not an enterprise which is entirely theory-free (McLaughlin and Precians;[1] Naylor[2]). There are embedded assumptions concerning the nature of variables, and these involve implications for their operational definition and measurement. They are seen very clearly in the work which Cattell and Eysenck have inspired, since source traits and personality types are not reducible to the results of factor analysis; they involve additional psychological assumptions.

The notion of underachievement provides a point of departure for studying the effects of personality characteristics on achievement. However, the notion is not without its difficulties since it suggests that for the so-called underachiever there is a level of *possible* achievement which he is not attaining. This suggestion relies heavily on the empirical relationship between IQ and attainment, and yet that relationship is far from perfect. Any suggestion that it could or ought to be perfect is, of course, begging questions concerning performance determinants other than intelligence. Such a suggestion is challenged by the notion of overachievement. This notion is also reliant on the relationship between IQ and attainment, but the so-called overachiever is regarded as being less of a "case" than the underachiever. We have seen that IQ, when it is a measure of "pure" intelligence, typically accounts for about 25 per cent of the variance in attainment (Cattell;[3] Cattell, Sealey and Sweney[4]); so that even if there were no individual differences in intelligence, the individual differences in performance would still be 75 per cent of what they now are. It is therefore plausible to suggest that there are individual differences between pupils in characteristics other than intelligence which influence performance. The usefulness of the notions of under- and overachievement lies in their calling attention to the fact that individual differences in performance are not totally explained by individual differences in intelligence. It can easily be forgotten, however, that these notions are relative to the prediction of performance from intelligence, which is not and cannot be perfect. To regard such achievers as educational "problems" is to ignore the possibility that other variables may systematically affect performance.

The study by Oakland[5] indicates some of the possible correlates of under- and overachievement. In his sample, overachievers were better organised, and more motivated, cooperative and conformist than underachievers. Underachievers tended to be more impulsive, critical and angry, and avoided facing problems. The important aspect of these differentiating characteristics was their tendency to involve areas of activity in addition to schoolwork, thereby indicating that they were pervasive characteristics of the overachievers' and underachievers' personalities. It is also of interest that no indicators of pathology or disturbance distinguished the two groups. At least in Oakland's sample, then, the underachievers' lack of constructive approaches to schoolwork seems not to be associated with emotional tensions and conflict. If his results are representative of general trends, performance cannot be maximised unless the conditions for learning are changed. Changes in the personalities of underachievers in the direction of more organisation of work and increased motivation to succeed is an immediately desirable goal, but such desirability does not constitute a recipe for its achievement. Perhaps a more feasible alternative would be to structure the learning environment in ways which minimise the effects of such characteristics on attainment. Programmed learning (Skinner[6]), and its more recent first cousin, computer-based instruction, hold great promise for coping with individual differences among pupils because the learning environment can be adapted to these differences. Gaudry and Spielberger[7] discuss its effects in alleviating the effects of anxiety on performance; and conceivably the negative effects of other personal characteristics, such as the lack of a capacity for organisation of work, can be similarly mitigated.

Studies of the relation between adjustment and attainment do not present a clear picture. The notion of adjustment as a global personal quality has been severely criticised (Cox[8]), and it has been suggested that there may be particular adjustments to particular situations— academic, family, peer-group—which are quite independent of one another. On the other hand, Matlin and Mendelsohn[9] found that when the effects of intelligence were held constant, adjustment measures were related to teachers' ratings of performance. Naylor and Gaudry[10] argued that the operational definitions of adjustment used in many studies were implicitly normative, and thereby subject to the effects of social desirability response sets (Edwards[11]). They also contended that the construct of adjustment tended to become confused with measures of other psychological constructs, particularly anxiety. They used a measure of adjustment derived from the semantic differential technique (Osgood, Suci and Tannenbaum[12]) which, they held, minimised the effects of social desirability, and was not reducible to measures of other psychological constructs. They found that this measure of adjustment was significantly related to performance in mathematics independent of the effects of anxiety and intelligence. Their results were consistent with the global adjustment position, but their study requires replication so that the relation between their adjustment measure and performance in other school subjects can be established. It is also of interest that their results are consistent with the findings concerning the relation between stability and performance in first year secondary school. Since the measures of stability are normative, and if there is a true positive relation between neuroticism and attainment at higher educational levels, it is possible that at these higher levels the Naylor and Gaudry measure would be more consistent with neuroticism than stability. This would depend on the maintenance of the significant relation between their measure of adjustment and performance at these levels. In so far as their measure of adjustment is a more subtle and sensitive measure than normative measures, there may well be important theoretical implications in their results for the relation between personality characteristics and academic attainment. In terms of their measure, the global adjustment position (e.g. Rogers[13, 14, 15]) may yet contribute to our understanding of the determinants of performance.

The study by Everett[16] provides a basis for characterising the self-concepts of high, medium and low achievers among a sample of university students. Further work is needed to determine the applicability of these characterisations at other levels of education. However, both his method and his results reveal new ways of tackling difficult problems.

Studies of the relation between Cattells's source traits and academic performance show trends that are apparently consistent with some of the findings in the underachievement and adjustment areas. At least the results suggest that some of the findings can be similarly interpreted. In particular Cattell's factors G (conscientiousness) and Q3 (self-sufficiency) bear conceptual similarity to Oakland's organisation-of-work variable and Naylor and Gaudry's adjustment variable. In all cases these are positively related to achievement, although this is not a ground for suggesting that measures of the variables are equivalent. Together, however, they do make psychological sense and are indicative of possible pervasive relationships. The relation of Cattell's second-order factors of extraversion and anxiety to performance is important also. The finding that the high-anxious tend to be the worse performers accords with what appears to be the general trend in that relationship (Gaudry and Spielberger[7]). The positive correlations between extraversion and attainment, at least prior to secondary school, are consistent with the findings of studies inspired by Eysenck's theory: the stable extravert seems to have a distinct advantage in performance in primary school. Further studies of the primary factors' relations with performance are necessary to establish their usefulness in the prediction and explanation of school performance. No doubt this will necessitate the development of tests containing more items to measure factors which appear to be critical.

The results of studies concerning the relation between achievement and Eysenck's factors of introversion-extraversion and neuroticism present a complex picture. Apparent age trends suggest that the better performers are stable extraverts in primary school and neurotic introverts in the university. The reasons for this trend are far from clear; and, particularly at the early age levels, seem not to be in accordance with Eysenck's theory of conditionability (Eysenck[17]). The picture is further complicated by the apparent sex differences which emerge in secondary school. Whether or not introverts are "late developers", as Eysenck and Cookson[18] suggest, and whether or not such late development is sex-linked, as their results and those of Entwistle and Cunningham[19] suggest, bear further investigation. A major issue in all the studies derived from this framework concerns the empirical stability of the *N and I-E* factors. It is possible that the stable extraverted high performer in primary school becomes the neurotic introverted high performer in the university. The findings of Savage[20] complicate the matter further at the university level. Even though his students were on average more neurotic than the general community, there appeared to be an optimum level of neuroticism such that extremely high neurotics performed more poorly than the rest. The complexity of these trends suggest the need for a longitudinal study to find out the true nature of the situation.

From time to time throughout this book, reference has been made to the nature of school organisation and functioning, and its possible influence on performance. No data which bear on this issue have been presented here, but its effects are doubtless of tremendous importance. Schools probably influence and mould personalities in ways which either facilitate or impede school performance. We have seen that sex differences in attainment can be affected by the sex of the teacher (Meyer and Thompson[21]), and that changes in the medium of instruction can affect the advantages which girls have in learning to read (McNeil[22]). Thus any educational disadvantages which accrue from the possession of particular personality characteristics may not be immutable. The positive utilisation of personality characteristics in the interests of learning, however, will no doubt require not only extensive research, but the development of a more flexible and adaptable school organisation.

The research reviewed in this book indicates that general assertions concerning the relation between personality and academic achievement are unlikely to have general validity. On these grounds it is also unlikely that the transient fashions in education attempting to promote "growth", "discovery learning", and so on will make a lasting contribution to the development of the learning environment most appropriate for each child. The psychologist considers empirical research of indisputable importance here. Hopefully the professional teacher will be aware of the necessity for such research and be prepared to cooperate in it.

References

[1] R. McLaughlin and R. Precians, "Educational Psychology: Some Questions of Status", in R. J. W. Selleck (Ed.), *Melbourne Studies in Education*, Melbourne University Press, Melbourne, 1969.

[2] F. D. Naylor, "Some Problems in the Relation Between Psychology and Educational Psychology", *Educational Philosophy and Theory*, 1971, **3**, pp. 47-53.

[3] R. B. Cattell, *The Scientific Analysis of Personality*, Penguin, Harmondsworth, 1965.

[4] R. B. Cattell, A. P. Sealey and A. B. Sweney, "What can Personality and Motivation Source Trait Measurements Add to the Prediction of School Achievement?", *British Journal of Educational Psychology*, 1966, **36**, pp. 280-95.

[5] J. A. Oakland, "Measurement of Personality Correlates of Academic Achievement in High School Students", *Journal of Counseling Psychology*, 1969, **16**, pp. 452-57.

[6] B. F. Skinner, *Cumulative Record* (enlarged ed.), Appleton-Century-Crofts, New York, 1961.

[7] E. Gaudry and C. D. Spielberger, *Anxiety and Educational Achievement*, John Wiley & Sons, Sydney, 1971.

[8] F. N. Cox, "Academic and Social Adjustment in 5th Grade Boys", *Australian Journal of Education*, 1961, **5**, pp. 185-92.

[9] A. H. Matlin and F. A. Mendelsohn, "The Relationship between Personality and Achievement Variables in the Elementary School", *Journal of Educational Research*, 1965, **58**, pp. 457-59.

[10] F. D. Naylor and E. Gaudry, "The Relationship of Adjustment, Anxiety and Intelligence to Mathematics Performance", *Journal of Educational Research* (in press).

[11] A. L. Edwards, *The Social Desirability Variable in Personality Assessment and Research*, Dryden Press, New York, 1957.

[12] C. E. Osgood, G. Suci and P. Tannenbaum, *The Measurement of Meaning*, University of Illinois Press, Urbana, 1957.

[13] C. R. Rogers, *Client-Centered Therapy*, Houghton Mifflin, Boston, 1951.

[14] C. R. Rogers, *On Becoming a Person*, Constable, London, 1961.

[15] C. R. ROGERS, *Freedom to Learn*, C. E. Merrill, Columbus, 1969.

[16] A. V. EVERETT, "The Self Concept of High, Medium and Low Academic Achievers", *Australian Journal of Education*, 1971, **15**, pp. 319-24.

[17] H. J. EYSENCK, *The Dynamics of Anxiety and Hysteria*, Routledge and Kegan Paul, London, 1957.

[18] H. J. EYSENCK and D. COOKSON, "Personality in Primary School Children: 1. Ability and Achievement", *British Journal of Educational Psychology*, 1969, **39**, pp. 109-30.

[19] N. J. ENTWISTLE and SHIRLEY CUNNINGHAM, "Neuroticism and School Attainment—A Linear Relationship?" *British Journal of Educational Psychology*, 1968, **38**, pp. 123-32.

[20] R. D. SAVAGE, "Personality Factors and Academic Performance", *British Journal of Educational Psychology*, 1962, **32**, pp. 251-53.

[21] W. J. MEYER and G. C. THOMPSON, "Sex Difference in the Distribution of Teacher Approval and Disapproval Among Sixth Grade Children", *Journal of Educational Psychology*, 1959, **47**, pp. 385-96.

[22] J. D. McNEIL, "Programed Instruction as a Research Tool in Reading: An Annotated Case", *Journal of Programed Instruction*, 1962, **1**, pp. 37-42.

Part Two
Selected Readings

Chapter 8

Teachers' Expectancies: Determinants of Pupils' IQ Gains

ROBERT ROSENTHAL
Harvard University

LENORE JACOBSON
*South San Francisco
Unified School District*

Within each of 18 classrooms, an average of 20 per cent of the children were reported to classroom teachers as showing unusual potential for intellectual gains. Eight months later these "unusual" children (who had actually been selected at random) showed significantly greater gains in IQ than did the remaining children in the control group. These effects of teachers' expectancies operated primarily among the younger children.

Experiments have shown that in behavioural research employing human or animal Ss, E's expectancy can be a significant determinant of S's response. (Rosenthal.[1,5]) In studies employing animals, for example, Es led to believe that their rat Ss had been bred for superior learning ability obtained performance superior to that obtained by Es led to believe their rats had been bred for inferior learning ability (Rosenthal and Fode,[2] Rosenthal and Lawson[3]). The present study was designed to extend the generality of this finding from Es to teachers and from animal Ss to school children.

This research was supported by Research Grants GS-177 and GS-714 from Division of Social Sciences of the National Science Foundation. The authors thank Dr. Paul Nielsen, Superintendent, South San Francisco Unified School District, for making this study possible; Dr. David Marlowe for his valuable advice; and Mae Evans, Nancy Johnson, John Laszlo, Susan Novick, and George Smiltens for their assistance.

Reprinted with permission of author and publisher: Rosenthal, R., and Jacobson, L. Teachers' expectancies: determinants of pupils' IQ gains. *Psychological Reports*, 1966, **19**, pp. 115-18.

Flanagan[4] has developed a nonverbal intelligence test (*Tests of General Ability* or *TOGA*) which is not explicitly dependent on such school-learned skills as reading, writing, and arithmetic. The test is composed of two types of items, "verbal" and "reasoning". The "verbal" items measure the child's level of information, vocabulary, and concepts. The "reasoning" items measure the child's concept formation ability by employing abstract line drawings. Flanagan's purpose in developing the TOGA was "to provide a relatively fair measure of intelligence for all individuals, even those who have had atypical opportunities to learn" (Flanagan,[4] p. 6).

Flanagan's test was administered to all children in an elementary school, disguised as a test designed to predict academic "blooming" or intellectual gain. Within each of the six grades in the school were three classrooms, one each of children performing at above average, average, and below average levels of scholastic achievement. In each of the 18 classes an average of 20 per cent of the children were assigned to the experimental condition. The names of these children were given to each teacher who was told that their scores on the "test for intellectual blooming" indicated that they would show unusual intellectual gains during the academic year. Actually, the children had been assigned to the experimental condition by means of a table of random numbers. The experimental treatment for these children, then, consisted of nothing more than being identified to their teachers as children who would show unusual intellectual gains.

Eight months after the experimental conditions were instituted all children were retested with the same IQ test and a change score was computed for each child. Table 8.1 shows the mean gain in IQ points among experimental and control Ss in each of the six grades.* For the school as a whole those children from whom the teachers had been led to expect greater intellectual gain showed a significantly greater gain in IQ score than did the control children ($p = 0 \cdot 02$, one-tail). Inspection

TABLE 8.I
Mean Gains in IQ

Grade	Controls		Experimentals		Diff-	t	$p\dagger$
	M	σ	M	σ	erence		
1	12·0	16·6	27·4	12·5	15·4	2·97	0·002
2	7·0	10·0	16·5	18·6	9·5	2·28	0·02
3	5·0	11·9	5·0	9·3	0·0		
4	2·2	13·4	5·6	11·0	3·4		
5	17·5	13·1	17·4	17·8	−0·1		
6	10·7	10·0	10·0	6·5	−0·7		
Weighted M	8·4 *	13·5	12·2 * *	15·0	3·8	2·15	0·02

* Mean number of children per grade = 42·5.
** Mean number of children per grade = 10·8.
† p one-tailed.

* There were no differences in the effects of teachers' expectancies as a function of S's initial level of educational achievement; therefore, the three classrooms at each grade level were combined for Table 8.1. In one of the three classrooms at the fifth grade level, a portion of the IQ test was inadvertently not re-administered so that data of Table 8.1 are based on 17 instead of 18 classrooms.

of Table 8.1 shows that the effects of teachers' expectancies were not uniform across the six grade levels. The lower the grade level, the greater was the effect ($rho = -0.94$, $p = 0.02$, two-tail). It was in the first and second grades that the effects were most dramatic. The largest gain among the three first grade classrooms occurred for experimental Ss who gained 24·8 IQ points *in excess* of the gain ($+16.2$) shown by the controls. The largest gain among the three second grade classrooms was obtained by experimental Ss who gained 18·2 IQ points in excess of the gain ($+4.3$) shown by the controls.

An additionally useful way of showing the effects of teachers' expectancies on their pupils' gains in IQ is to show the percentage of experimental and control Ss achieving various magnitudes of gains. Table 8.2 shows such percentages for the first and second grades only.

TABLE 8.2

Percentages of Experimental and Control Ss Gaining 10, 20, or 30 IQ Points (First and Second Grade Children)

IQ Gain	Control Ss*	Experimental Ss**	χ^2	p†
10 points	49	79	4·75	0·02
20 points	19	47	5·59	0·01
30 points	5	21	3·47	0·04

* Total number of children = 95.
** Total number of children = 19.
†p one-tailed.

Half again as many experimental as control Ss gained at least 10 IQ points; more than twice as many gained at least 20 IQ points; and more than four times as many gained at least 30 points.

An important question was whether the gains of the experimental Ss were made at the expense of the control Ss. Tables 8.1 and 8.2 show that control Ss made substantial gains in IQ though they were smaller than the gains made by experimental Ss. Better evidence for the proposition that gains by experimental Ss were not made at the expense of control Ss comes from the positive correlation between gains made by experimental and control Ss. Over the 17 classrooms in which the comparison was possible, those in which experimental Ss made greater gains tended also to be the ones where control Ss made greater gains ($rho = 0.57$, $p = 0.02$, two-tail).

Retesting of the children's IQ had been done in classroom groups by the children's own teacher.* The question arose, therefore, whether the greater gain in IQ of the experimental children might have been due to the teacher's differential behaviour toward them during the retesting. To help answer this question three of the classes were retested by a school administrator not attached to the particular school. She did not know which children were in the experimental condition. Results based on her retesting of the children were not significantly different from the results based on the children's own teachers' retesting. In fact, there was a tendency for the results of her retesting to yield even larger

* Scoring of the tests was done by the investigators, not by the teachers.

effects of teachers' expectancies. It appears unlikely, then, that the greater IQ gains made by children from whom greater gains were expected could be attributed to the effect of the behaviour of the teacher while she served as an examiner.

There are a number of possible explanations of the finding that teachers' expectancy effects operated primarily at the lower grade levels, including: (a) Younger children have less well-established reputations so that the creation of expectations about their performance would be more credible. (b) Younger children may be more susceptible to the unintended social influence exerted by the expectation of their teacher. (c) Younger children may be more recent arrivals in the school's neighbourhood and may differ from the older children in characteristics other than age. (d) Teachers of lower grades may differ from teachers of higher grades on a variety of dimensions which are correlated with the effectiveness of the unintentional communication of expectancies.

The most important question which remains is that which asks how a teacher's expectation becomes translated into behaviour in such a way as to elicit the expected pupil behaviour. Prior research on the unintentional communication of expectancies in experimentally more carefully controlled interactions suggests that this question will not be easily answered (Rosenthal[1]).

But, regardless of the mechanism involved, there are important substantive and methodological implications of these findings which will be discussed in detail elsewhere. For now, one example, in question form, will do: How much of the improvement in intellectual performance attributed to the contemporary educational programmes is due to the content and methods of the programmes and how much is due to the favourable expectancies of the teachers and administrators involved? Experimental designs to answer such questions are available (Rosenthal[1]) and in view of the psychological, social and economic importance of these programmes the use of such designs seems strongly indicated.

References

[1] R. ROSENTHAL, *Experimenter Effects in Behavioral Research*, Appleton-Century-Crofts, New York, 1966.

[2] R. ROSENTHAL and K. L. FODE, "The effect of experimenter bias on the performance of the albino rat", *Behavioral Science*, 1963, **8**, 83-89.

[3] R. ROSENTHAL and R. LAWSON, "A longitudinal study of the effects of experimenter bias on the operant learning of laboratory rats", *Journal of Psychiatric Research*, 1964, **2**, 61-72.

[4] J. C. FLANAGAN, *Tests of General Ability: Technical Report*, Science Research Associates, Chicago, 1960.

[5] R. ROSENTHAL, "The effect of the experimenter on the results of psychological research", in B. A. Maher (Ed.), *Progress in Experimental Personality Research*, Vol. I, Academic Press, New York, 1964, pp. 79-114.

Chapter 9

Measurement of Personality Correlates of Academic Achievement in High School Students

JAMES A. OAKLAND
University of Washington School of Medicine

This study attempted to use more refined methodological and measurement techniques to help clarify some of the problems in the area of scholastic underachievement. The Edwards Personality Inventory (EPI) was administered to 241 high school juniors, and scores were correlated with underachievement defined as the discrepancy between predicted and obtained scholastic performance. Performance was measured by grade-point average (GPA); ability, by Differential Aptitude Test (DAT). GPA was predicted from the regression of obtained GPA on DAT. Underachievement correlated with 16 EPI scales for males, 10 for females, with magnitudes ranging to 0·52 (males) and 0·35 (females). Traits related to broadly generalised work habits, attitudinal and motivational factors, and social conformity.

That academic achievement and underachievement have been the object of intensive interest and concern is attested by the profusion of studies in this area as well as the opinion of those working with adolescents in educational, medical, and psychiatric settings (see Kornrich,[1] Lavin,[2] Raph, Goldbert, and Passow,[3] Thorndike,[4] etc., for reviews of

This study was a portion of a doctoral dissertation completed at the University of Washington, 1967. Grateful acknowledgements are extended to Allen L. Edwards for his invaluable assistance; to the Seattle, Washington school district for their cooperation; to Alan Klockars and Gordon Cochrane for assistance in calculations and socioeconomic status judgments. This research was supported in part by Research Grant MH-04075 from the National Institute of Mental Health, United States Public Health Service, Allen L. Edwards, principal investigator.

studies in this area). Unfortunately, the quality of the research has not kept pace with the quantity. Raph and Tannenbaum,[5] in a frequently cited review of the literature on underachievement, report the findings to be "conflicting and inconclusive" and conclude "that despite the voluminous work done in this area, we do not as yet have a clear profile of traits that distinguishes underachievers, from their comparably able peers who live up to scholastic expectations [p. 138]." In accounting for this state of affairs, two problems stand out, namely, inadequate experimental design and inadequacies in the instruments used to quantify the variables of interest, particularly when these are personality traits.

Thorndike,[4] concerned with the first, worked out more adequate experimental designs for those working in this area. The present study uses his design as a basis. The second problem can be solved only as increasing sophistication in the development of personality measures results in new and more adequate instruments.

It is felt that such an instrument is found in the Edwards Personality Inventory (EPI) (Edwards[6]), a questionnaire developed over the past several years in response to the need for a personality inventory measuring a broader array of traits and less affected by response sets and other problems characterising objective measures of personality. Edwards accumulated a very large item pool by recording statements used by people in describing themselves and others, eliminated those statements having highly socially desirable or undesirable scale values and those eliciting an extremely large percentage of either true or false responses, and used extensive statistical analyses of the responses of some 750 college students to derive the resulting 53 scales scored from the 1,500 items in the inventory. These scales deal with a very broad range of everyday behaviour, but not that associated with psychiatric symptoms, religious and political beliefs, or other areas of private concern. The advantages in gaining cooperation from persons taking this inventory, while not arousing "defensiveness" are obvious, and the results obtained on individual *S*s are quite likely more usable samples of behaviour for personality research than those obtained from other personality inventories. It was felt that this inventory could be used with advantage in the study of academic underachievement.

Method

Over- and underachievement are defined as scholastic performances which are more or less than predicted on the basis of some aptitude measure. Predictions in the present study were made from the combined scores of the verbal reasoning and numerical ability subtests of the Differential Aptitude Test (Form L). This score correlates highly with standard intelligence tests and has consistently high test-retest reliability coefficients (Bennett, Seashore, and Wesman[7]).

The criterion was the overall grade-point average (GPA) obtained by the student during his sophomore and junior (autumn semester) years. While a number of problems have been cited with regard to the use of GPA (Thorndike[4]), it was used in this study because no other measure has successfully been proposed to replace it, because it is the measure which the school administrator is most interested in predicting, it is the typically used measure of academic achievement in the underachievement literature, and it is easily obtainable.

Socioeconomic status (SES), which has sometimes correlated with underachievement, was incorporated as a control variable, and estimated from the Hollingshead "Two-Factor Index of Social Position" (Hollingshead,[8] Myers and Roberts[9]), based on the personal data sheets filled out by the students.

Two hundred and forty-one students from two Seattle, Washington high schools completed the questionnaire. Both schools are in very similar, suburban, generally middle-class neighbourhoods within the city limits. Students were solicited from the junior class to minimise age differences, and to have a relatively stable high school GPA available. An honorarium was given for class activities and projects as an incentive for their participation in this project. Students participating were administered the EPI booklets A, C, D, and E, and the personal data sheet (Booklet B, containing alternate forms of the scales in A, was omitted because of the amount of time involved). Standard instructions were used and answers were recorded on IBM answer sheets. The four booklets were finished by each student within 2 weeks; most were finished within 4 days. Since it was noted in the first high school that about twice as many girls as boys tended to volunteer for the project, every effort was made in the second high school to recruit boys, which resulted in better balance. Table 9.1 gives a description of the sample and compares the students who participated with those in the entire junior class.

Although every effort possible was made to involve a maximum number of students, only about one-fourth of the class responded. This was largely due to the length of the test and to the other demands on the students' time, for example, after-school jobs. The degree of resemblance of samples to the class, however, suggests that the selective factors operating were not too grossly distorting with regard to the variables listed. Certainly, as may have been predicted, the better students tended to respond more than poorer students, and girls more than boys. Nevertheless, the sample does include a relatively wide range of aptitude, achievement, and SES level.

Over- and underachievement were measured by a "discrepancy score", that is, the obtained GPA minus the predicted GPA estimated from the regression of obtained GPA on DAT, separately by sex and school (Thorndike[4]). The primary interest of this study is in the correlations between this discrepancy score and the 53 EPI scales. However, it was anticipated that these correlations might differ significantly for different levels of aptitude, that they might be confounded by SES, and that the variables might not be related linearly. Consequently, the following additional analyses were made, all separately for each sex; the sample was divided into two levels of aptitude (at the median) and correlations rerun. These were inspected for linearity. The relationship

TABLE 9.1

Comparison of Students Participating with Those in the Entire Junior Class

Item	Male		Female	
	Sample	Class	Sample	Class
Students				
No. in high school "A"	44	360	93	316
No. in high school "B"	54	304	50	268
Total N	98		143	
Grade-point average				
High school "A"				
$\overline{X}$	2·781	2·192	2·953	2·569
SD	0·637	0·723	0·595	0·693
High school "B"				
$\overline{X}$	2·407	2·072	2·636	2·455
SD	0·743	0·766	0·632	0·760
Differential Aptitude Test				
High school "A"				
$\overline{X}$	56·95	48·63	57·04	50·97
SD	14·35	14·20	13·29	15·62
High school "B"				
$\overline{X}$	53·13	48·17	53·52	50·47
SD	14·17	13·56	13·19	15·24
Age				
$\overline{X}$	16·81		16·81	
SD	0·38		0·32	
Socioeconomic status				
I	9%		13%	
II	19%		23%	
III	46%		40%	
IV	23%		24%	
V	3%		4%	

between these variables and SES was then observed and partial correlations (partialling out SES) were computed where necessary.

Results

All tests of significance were carried out at the 0·01 level (two-tailed tests) since the large number of variables involved in this study made it more likely that some variables would reach significance by chance. Means and standard deviations for each of the scales are reported elsewhere (Oakland[10]). Table 9.2 presents the correlations between the discrepancy scores as a measure of over- and underachievement, and the various EPI scales, both for the complete sample by sex, and after it is split into two levels of aptitude.

TABLE 9.2

**Correlations between Over-, Underachievement and
53 Edwards Personality Inventory Scales**

Booklet	Male sample	High-aptitude males	Low-aptitude males	Female sample	High-aptitude females	Low-aptitude females
A 1. Plans and Organises Things	0·471*	0·496*	0·446*	0·262*(0·222)	0·177	0·322*(0·280)
2. Intellectually Oriented	0·294*	0·172	0·359	0·058	0·103	—0·017
3. Persistent	0·365*	0·280	0·444*	0·164	0·166	0·153
4. Self-Confident	0·314*	0·287	0·316	0·140	0·000	0·264
5. Cultural Interests	0·166	0·224	0·044	0·006	0·051	—0·070
6. Centre of Attention	—0·053	—0·117	0·017	—0·070	—0·142	—0·017
7. Carefree	0·211	0·135	0·298	0·039	—0·111	0·185
8. Conformity	0·260*	0·220	0·326	0·215*	0·194	0·258
9. Leadership	0·329*	0·281	0·354	0·139	0·058	0·207
10. To Be Kind to Others	0·108	0·064	0·151	—0·045	—0·136	0·041
11. To Worry about Making a Good Impression	0·154	0·128	0·170	0·012	—0·140	0·162
12. Impulsive	—0·026	—0·145	0·089	—0·249*	—0·257	—0·247
13. To Like to Be Alone	—0·093	—0·124	—0·107	0·045	0·005	0·048
14. Interest in the Behaviour of Others	0·166	0·106	0·200	—0·035	—0·033	—0·058
C 1. Anxiety about Competition	0·065	0·055	0·102	0·063	0·091	0·047
2. Avoids Facing Problems	—0·318*	—0·248	—0·362	—0·240*	—0·162	—0·303
3. Perfectionist	0·501*	0·497*	0·494*	0·239*(0·197)	0·090	0·362*(0·325)
4. Absent-Minded	—0·116	—0·073	—0·155	—0·250*	—0·164	—0·343*
5. Sensitivity to Criticism	—0·187	—0·242	—0·152	—0·043	—0·064	—0·007
6. To Like a Set Routine	0·113	—0·091	0·281	0·098	0·082	0·137
7. To Want Sympathy	0·033	—0·151	0·179	—0·039	—0·011	—0·082
8. Avoids Arguments	—0·107	—0·227	—0·006	—0·008	—0·012	0·018
9. Unemotional	—0·129	—0·215	—0·041	—0·107	—0·117	—0·099
10. Easily Influenced	—0·199	—0·297	—0·105	—0·050	—0·104	0·008
11. Misunderstood	—0·214	—0·283	—0·147	—0·145	—0·177	—0·103
D 1. To Be Motivated to Succeed	0·463*	0·342	0·568*	0·125	0·004	0·250
2. To Be Impressed by Status	0·150	0·073	0·211	—0·058	—0·024	—0·095
3. To Desire Recognition	0·203	0·200	0·221	0·024	0·012	0·032
4. Plans Work Efficiently	0·522*	0·536*	0·507*	0·347*	0·290	0·396*
5. To Cooperate with a Group	0·411*	0·370	0·461*	0·118	0·056	0·178
6. Competitive	0·404*	0·404*	0·409*	0·037	0·051	0·021
7. To Be Articulate	0·241	0·283	0·176	0·072	0·060	0·064
8. To Feel Superior	0·013	0·088	—0·062	—0·060	—0·105	—0·030
9. To Be Logical	0·262*	0·120	0·373*	0·098	0·073	0·109
10. To Assume Responsibility	0·427*	0·400*	0·442*	0·188	0·173	0·196
11. Self-Centred	—0·150	—0·214	—0·075	—0·063	—0·064	—0·042
12. To Make Friends Easily	0·225	0·152	0·334	0·041	—0·044	0·147
13. To Say What One Thinks	0·026	0·168	—0·086	—0·009	—0·027	0·013
14. To Be a Dependable Worker	0·435*	0·453*	0·436*	—0·282*	0·163	0·401*(0·367)
15. To Be Neat in Dress	0·152	0·236	0·089	—0·029	—0·067	0·035
E 1. To Be Self-Critical	—0·220	—0·265	—0·146	—0·094	—0·075	—0·102
2. To Be Critical of Others	0·075	0·197	—0·012	—0·264*	—0·191	—0·337*
3. To Be Active	0·065	0·074	0·109	0·002	—0·137	0·123
4. To Talk about Oneself	0·236	0·225	0·269	0·004	0·038	—0·038
5. To Become Angry	0·176	0·068	0·302	—0·207*	—0·140	—0·283
6. To Help Others	0·219	0·182	0·275	0·051	—0·023	0·138
7. To Be Careful about One's Possessions	0·013	—0·042	0·091	0·148	0·060	0·238
8. To Understand Oneself	0·335*	0·221	0·428*	0·066	0·024	0·091
9. To Be Considerate of Others	0·255	0·170	0·315	0·117	0·054	0·188
10. To Be Dependent on Others	0·228	0·140	0·321	0·005	0·100	—0·110
11. To Be Shy	—0·241	—0·238	—0·254	—0·082	—0·139	—0·020
12. To Be Informed about Current Affairs	0·207	0·267	0·120	0·133	0·069	0·196
13. Virtuousness	0·097	0·136	0·099	0·109	0·008	0·211

* $p < 0·01$ (two-tailed test).

Nonlinearity did not characterise any of the relationships between discrepancy and EPI variables. SES was uncorrelated with discrepancy for males making a partial correlation unnecessary. For females, five correlations were recalculated partialling out SES; these are shown in parentheses in Columns 4 and 6. (For all other significant correlations, partialling out SES made minor or no variation.) Of the five partial correlations, only one was nonsignificant.

Discussion

One of the clusters of traits which has been most consistently related to underachievement in what Raph *et al.*[3] simply summarise as poor work habits and study skills, a finding which is confirmed and spelled out more clearly in this study. An examination of the scales which are most highly correlated with over- and underachievement (Plans Work Efficiently, Perfectionist, Plans and Organises Things, and To Be a Dependable Worker) reveals that while many items would be directly related to school work, for example, to have an assignment completed before it is due, to waste little time in getting down to work, to seldom be satisfied with the first draft of a paper, to plan work carefully, to work hard without supervision, etc., there are also many items which do not specifically apply to school work, for example, to keep things neat and orderly, to demand perfection in everything one does, to not be a lazy person, to enjoy being assigned to plan something, to enjoy planning the details of a holiday or vacation, etc. This suggests that these traits which are related to achievement are broadly generalised to many areas of personality functioning rather than specific to those work habits associated with school assignments. The fact that the scales have relatively high internal consistency would support this. If this is correct, and if the relationship is cause and effect as appears likely, it would be of interest to the parent and educator to assist the child or student toward developing a life-style characterised by this cluster of traits, in so far as one were aiming toward a goal of achievement.

Another cluster of traits correlates moderately well with the measure of over- and underachievement for males, namely, To Be Motivated to Succeed, To Assume Responsibility, Competitive, Persistent, Self-Confident, and Leadership. This is also suggestive of a generalised style of life but with the emphasis on one's attitudes and motivation. These are also characteristics more typically ascribed to males than females in our society, which may in part account for the lack of significant correlations for females on most of these scales.

Two scales, correlated with over-and underachievement but tapping traits somewhat different than those cited above, are To Cooperate with a Group and Conformity. A review of the items in these scales suggests a person who "fits in"; he respects tradition and authority, gets along with peers, accepts the group's standard, etc. This kind of student is obviously more appreciated by the average classroom teacher and this may be evidenced in the grades he receives.

Of the many scales which are significantly correlated with over- and underachievement, most are positive rather than negative traits. That there are no significant correlations with such scales as Anxiety about Competition, Sensitivity to Criticism, Misunderstood, To Be Self-Critical, or To Be Shy suggests that emotional conflicts and tensions may be less significant in diagnosing the problems of the underachiever than the relative absence of constructive approaches to the academic task coupled with the motivation and self-confidence to keep at it.

The scales which are significantly negatively correlated with over- and underachievement are: Avoids Facing Problems (males and females), and Absent-Minded, Impulsive, To be Critical of Others, and To Become Angry (females). Avoids Facing Problems appears to be a trait opposite the first cluster of characteristics discussed above. For example, some of the items are: to have to be reminded more than once about doing an unpleasant task, to put things off until the last minute, to avoid facing a problem as long as one possibly can, etc. "Impulsive" and "Absent-Minded" suggest a person who often behaves on impulse and who is characterised by a "flighty forgetfulness", and who, therefore, is also in contrast to the organised and purposeful person. The remaining pair, To be Critical of Others and To Become Angry, suggest the opposite of the person who "fits in" easily with others. Rather, he is critical of others, points out their mistakes, says things that irritate, and shows his anger easily especially in social situations.

That the size and number of significant correlations are greater for males is difficult to understand. Factors which may be involved include the differences in sex roles in our society, the possibility that those traits correlated with over-and underachievement for females are not measured by the EPI scales, or that this is a chance finding in this particular study and would not reoccur in a replication.

The division of the sample into high- and low-aptitude groups is a revealing one for many of the variables. The terms "high" and "low" aptitude are somewhat misleading, however. The division was at the median, but in terms of the national norms, this means that the high-aptitude group is in the top quartile of the national sample and that the low-aptitude group represents largely the middle range of aptitude with a few representatives from the lower ranges. Correlations between over- and underachievement and those EPI scales associated with efficient and purposeful planning and execution of tasks are of about the same magnitude for both the low-middle- and high-aptitude groups. However, the low-middle group shows higher correlations with the cluster of positive "attitudinal" traits and those associated with conformity and acceptance of tradition and authority, while high-aptitude students show some tendency to have higher correlations between underachievement and negative traits such as Sensitivity to Criticism, Easily Influenced, Misunderstood, and To Be Self-Critical (these are not significant at the 0.01 level but are in the expected direction, and are much more characteristic for males than females). An interpretation might be that all students need a style of life characterised by dependability, efficient and purposeful planning, and reasonably high goals if they are to achieve academically. In addition, students with average intellect are in need of the traits of persistence and self-confidence if they are to achieve, while the students with superior aptitude can rely on their intellectual abilities to get them well along toward achievement unless subverted by emotional conflicts and problems.

This set of correlates with academic over- and underachievement, while stating nothing about causation, serves as "an important first step to understanding causes" (cf. Thorndike[4]). Further steps may take several directions such as a more intensive study of what is being measured by the EPI scales, particularly those cited above. It would be of interest to determine when these traits appear in the student's development and what are other behavioural and attitudinal correlates of them. Are they particularly related to measurable characteristics of the home environment? EPI data from parents of underachievers would be highly interesting. Another direction for research would be to make a systematic attempt to change the characteristic presumed to be measured by the above scales, to see if changes in scores on these scales were related to changes on the over- and underachievement continuum.

References

[1] M. KORNRICH (Ed.), *Underachievement*, Charles C. Thomas, Springfield, 1965.

[2] D. LAVIN, *The Prediction of Academic Performance*, Russell Sage, New York, 1965.

[3] J. B. RAPH, M. L. GOLDBERT, and A. H. PASSOW, *Bright Underachievers*, Teachers College Press, Columbia University, New York, 1966.

[4] R. L. THORNDIKE, *The Concepts of Over- and Underachievement*, Teachers College Press, Columbia University, New York, 1963.

[5] J. B. RAPH and A. TANNENBAUM, Underachievement: Review of the literature. Unpublished manuscript, 1961. Cited by A. T. Jersild, *The Psychology of Adolescence*, 2nd Ed., Macmillan, New York, 1963.

[6] A. L. EDWARDS, *Manual for the Edwards Personality Inventory*, Science Research, Chicago, 1968.

[7] G. K. BENNETT, H. G. SEASHORE and A. G. WESMAN, *Manual for the Differential Aptitude Tests*, 4th Ed., Forms L and M, Psychological Corp., New York, 1966.

[8] A. B. HOLLINGSHEAD, *Elmtown's Youth: The Impact of Social Classes on Adolescents*, John Wiley & Sons, New York, 1949.

[9] J. K. MYERS and B. H. ROBERTS, *Family and Class Dynamics in Mental Illness*, John Wiley & Sons, New York, 1959.

[10] J. A. OAKLAND, "The Performance of High School Students on the Edwards Personality Inventory and its Relationship to Over- and Underachievement." Doctoral dissertation, University of Washington, Ann Arbor, 1968, University Microfilms, No. 68-3868.

Chapter 10

Academic and Social Adjustments in Fifth Grade Boys

F. N. COX
University of Melbourne

In recent years the concept of unitary or global adjustment, with its ambitious, if not pretentious, goal of "consideration of the whole personality of the pupil in its total environment" (Wright[1]), has been strongly criticised. The purposes of this paper are to discuss these criticisms, and to present some evidence pertaining to the relationship between academic and social adjustment in 5th grade boys.

Criticisms of Unitary or Global Adjustment

Adjustment is commonly defined in terms of freedom from tension, feelings of inner well-being and adapting oneself to the needs of other individuals. Writers (Coleman,[2] Rogers,[3] Sappenfield[4]) who define the term this way usually argue that these attributes are positively correlated, that adjustment is a unitary or global phenomenon. Several American sociologists (Lapiere,[5] Riesman,[6] Whyte[7]) have claimed that these conceptions of adjustment have had significant and, in their opinions, undesirable effects upon contemporary educational theory and practice in the United States. Their argument is that most educational theory and practice in America is based on the assumption that the prime purpose of education should be the integration and development of the whole individual into a well-rounded human being. Lapiere, Riesman and Whyte then suggest that this ideal of a "well-rounded

Based upon a thesis submitted to the University of Melbourne for the degree of Doctor of Philosophy.

From the *Australian Journal of Education*, 1961, **5**, pp. 184-92. Reprinted by permission of F. N. Cox and the Australian Council for Educational Research.

human being" means, in effect, a socially adjusted individual, a person who is free from tension, and who conforms to the wishes and needs of others. These and other writers (Becker and Boskoff,[8] Skinner[9]) then claim that implementation of these ideals have had three main effects on educational practice.

The first of these is stated to be training of "congenial, placid, uncompetitive individuals" (Lapiere,[5] p. 119). Next, it is claimed that teachers are "increasingly, young college graduates who have been taught to be more concerned with the child's social and psychological adjustment than with his academic progress—indeed, to scan the intellectual performance for signs of social maladjustment" (Riesman,[6] p. 60). More seriously, it is asserted that increasing inclusion of social adjustment courses is displacing parts of the traditional academic curriculum, and that the content of these courses in social adjustment is more than a little ludicrous. Examination of a primary source (Pierce[10]) provides some support for these criticisms. Two courses recently introduced include instruction on make-up and conversing on the telephone —the "rationale" for both being facilitation of student adjustment.

While it would obviously be foolish to suggest that these criticisms can be indiscriminately applied to all, or even the majority, of American schools, and while it would be absurd to argue that Australian educational theory and practice are vulnerable to such onslaughts, these sociologists do seem to be raising at least one important question. This can be posed in several ways: "Is adjustment unidimensional?" "Are academic and social adjustment positively correlated?" "Will improvement in a child's adjustment with his peers be associated with improvement in his academic performance?"

It is impossible, of course, to give unequivocal answers to questions of this kind. The kinds of answers that educational psychology can produce are necessarily limited ones: answers that are, or should be, restricted to carefully defined populations and to the particular measures used in a given study. Within these limits, however, it is possible to examine the relationship between academic and social adjustment and, thereby, to test the hypothesis that adjustment is a unitary or global phenomenon. In this deliberately restricted way, then, it is possible to make a partial test of the validity of one of the more basic assumptions of an educational philosophy.

The specific question to be posed for the remainder of this paper is: "Are academic and social adjustment positively correlated in 5th grade boys?" Possible answers will be sought from two sources: published empirical studies and an investigation recently undertaken in Melbourne.

Empirical Studies of Academic and Social Adjustment in Primary School Children

It is, perhaps, significant that there are remarkably few published studies of the relationship between measures of academic and social adjustment in primary school children. The comparative absence of reliable information may be one reason why there is so much emotion, so many black-and-white arguments and so much intolerance in debates about the number of dimensions of adjustment.

Several American studies (Bowman,[11] Buswell,[12] Kurtz and Swenson[13]) have reported positive correlations between various measures of academic and social adjustment. For example, Buswell, who made an analysis of the relationships between the social structure of the classroom and academic proficiency in eleven 5th grade classrooms in eight elementary (primary) schools, reported that "in general, those [children] who are succeeding in their school work will also be succeeding in their social relationships with their peers" (p. 51). In a study which is more directly concerned with individual behaviour, Bowman and his colleagues[11] reported some results of a long-term investigation into the conservation of mental health and the development of talent in a carefully specified population of 4th and 6th grade children in an Illinois city. Their measures included standardised ability and attainment tests, reputation scales for aggression, withdrawnness and social leadership, a sociometric status score, teachers' ratings and personal adjustment inventories. Their sample included both boys and girls, and contained children from intact and broken homes. Bowman *et al.* reported their findings in terms of three groups in which they were particularly interested: the aggressive, the withdrawn and the talented. From the quantitative and qualitative data they presented, it is clear that they found quite strong positive relationships between their measures of academic and social adjustment. This is particularly evident in the case of their "aggressive" and "withdrawn" children, who can validly be described as "generally maladjusted" on the basis of the evidence they presented in their monograph.

Design of the Melbourne Study

The present writer, however, has reported very different findings from a study (Cox[14]) of the relationship between academic and social adjustment in a sample of 5th grade boys from intact Melbourne families. This study will be described in some detail, and an attempt made to compare these findings with those reported by Bowman *et al.*, so that some inferences can be drawn concerning the conditions under which academic and social adjustment are, or are not, correlated in 5th grade children.

In 1956 the writer and others (Beswick,[15] Western[16]) began a series of investigations into selected aspects of the emotional, intellectual and social functioning of 5th grade boys who lived with both their parents in a suburb of Melbourne. This population was selected for several reasons. Underlying the selection of children from intact families was the conviction that far too much of our knowledge and speculation about child behaviour have been derived from clinical studies of emotionally, intellectually or socially deviant individuals or groups. Secondly, primary school children were chosen to ensure that the broad course of the children's school experiences would be approximately equivalent. Fifth grade children were selected because it was known (Herbst[17]) that most of them would be capable of writing answers to simply worded questions which they would have to read. Finally, the population was restricted to boys because it was thought that social relationships could be investigated more exhaustively if questions were confined to the activities of one sex.

The original *sample* comprised 519 boys who attended 16 schools from ecologically diverse areas of Melbourne. Incomplete test records and an unusually high incidence of absence from school due to a severe epidemic of "Asian flu" reduced this to an effective sample of 432 boys. From this effective sample 250 cases were selected for detailed analysis. This large sample was used for all analyses except for relationships to school examination performance. The subsample used to analyse the correlates of school examination marks will be described later.

The *measures* used can be grouped under five headings: sociological characteristics, family factors, personality variables, peer group evaluations and an estimate of academic proficiency.

The *sociological characteristics* assessed were father's occupation and the ecological area of the children's home. Occupations were classified in terms of levels of responsibility, education and personnel control. The suburbs in which the children lived were evaluated in terms of type of dwellings and extent of service facilities.

Four *family factors* were investigated (Cox and Leaper[18]). All four were concerned with children's reports of parent behaviours and children's reactions to these behaviours, and all are quite independent of each other. The variables were: Love, Social Restriction, Household Duties and Responsibilities and Family Cohesion. "Love" referred to the extent to which parent behaviour is child-oriented, developmentally relevant and child-respecting. "Social Restriction" was concerned with the extent to which parents confine their children's social relationships to specified places and permit them to associate only with approved persons. "Household Duties and Responsibilities" indicates the extent to which children participate in routine household tasks and/or accept responsibility for them. Finally, "Family Cohesion" measures the extent to which parents join together (with their children, where appropriate) in leisure activities in and outside their home.

The four *personality variables* studied were general and test anxiety (Sarason *et al.*[19]), achievement motivation (Cox[20]) and children's attitudes towards their parents (Cox[21]). Both anxieties were measured by means of personal inventories, and the other two variables were assessed by a projective technique—Murray's[22] Thematic Apperception Test. There were also four measures of *peer group evaluation*—a standard index of sociometric status and three reputation scales (Beswick and Cox[23]). These reputation scales were the frequencies with which children were stated by their peers to indulge in aggressive, dependent and immature behaviours.

An estimate of *academic proficiency* was derived from school examination marks. The children in this subsample of 96 cases came from five schools in which there were no significant differences between the means and standard deviations of examination marks in five basic subjects—Arithmetic, Composition, Grammar, Reading and Spelling. Since the distributions of these marks were similar, it was decided to combine them and so derive a single estimate of academic proficiency for the 96 children. It was appreciated that this procedure of combining examination marks from different schools was liable to introduce error because of possible differences in marking standards, but no other measure of academic proficiency was available.* The measure was regarded purely as an estimate, and composite marks were divided into two groups by splitting them at the median: that is, the measure was used to obtain only a general indication of academic proficiency. The consistency and significance of the results obtained with this measure seem to justify the procedure.

Finally, it should be mentioned that the statistical relationships which were found in the large sample of 250 boys also held for the subsample of 96 cases, so the academic proficiency sample was presumably representative of the larger one.

Findings

Statistical analysis of the pattern of interrelationships between these five groups of measures yielded the following findings (Cox[14], Chapter 7):

(i) There were two adjustment clusters—academic and social adjustment;

(ii) the clusters were independent of each other;

(iii) each cluster had its own specific family correlate;

(iv) neither cluster was correlated with the sociological characteristics assessed in this study.

The patterns of statistical relationships within and between the clusters are summarised in Table 10.1.

These findings are, then, clearly at variance with those reported by Bowman and his associates who, it will be recalled, found positive correlations between their measures of academic and social adjustment. While it is extremely difficult to make a detailed comparison of two studies conducted for different purposes on different populations, it does seem profitable to speculate about possible reasons for these varying results, when the children in both studies were similar in age and when some of the measures used were also rather similar.

Firstly, it may be significant that Bowman *et al.* reported that "withdrawn children, as screened by these tests, are more often girls than boys" (Bowman,[13] p. 31). Since the present writer did not study girls, it is possible that his correlations between academic and social adjustment were considerably reduced in size by the absence of girls. Again, Bowman reported that his aggressive boys "more often came from large families, many of which have been broken by separation or divorce"

---

* Since the children were examined for a total of over nine hours, it was impractical and unreasonable to request additional time to administer a series of attainment tests.

TABLE 10.1

Statistical Relationships between Measures of Academic and Social Adjustment

	Academic adjustment					Social adjustment			
	Test anxiety	General anxiety	Achievement motive	Household duties	School marks	Attitudes to parents	Love	Sociometric status	Reputed immaturity
Academic adjustment									
Test anxiety	—	X X	X	X	X X				
General anxiety	X X	—	X X		X				
Achievement motive	X	X X	—	X X	X X				
Household duties	X		X X	—	X				
School marks	X X	X	X X	X	—				
Social adjustment									
Attitudes to parents						—	X X	X X	X X
Love						X X	—	X	X X
Sociometric status						X X	X	—	X X
Reputed immaturity						X X	X X	X X	—

Notes; (a) X denotes statistical significance at 0·05 level.
  (b) X X denotes statistical significance at 0·01 level.
  (c) Absence of entries in upper right and lower left quadrants indicate independence of these measures of academic and social adjustment.

(Bowman,[13] p. 31). Since the Melbourne study was restricted to boys from intact families, the difference in the populations studied may account in part for the different findings. Apart from these population differences there remains, of course, the possibility of a wider cross-cultural difference between American and Australian children, but this speculation cannot be evaluated until carefully planned, comparable studies are conducted in both countries.

Some Implications of these Findings

It seems possible to draw some tentative conclusions from the findings presented above. Firstly, the size (and statistical significance) of correlation coefficients between measures of academic and social adjustment depend upon the nature of the population studied. If the population studied is defined to include all children of a specified age range, or if it is restricted to deviant, extreme groups of children (Goldfarb,[24] Terman[25]), then American findings are that measures of academic and social adjustment are positively correlated. This evidence, then, offers some support for the concept of unitary or global adjustment.

Conversely, if the population is limited to ten- to eleven-year-old boys from intact, urban families, Australian evidence shows that academic and social competence are two independent dimensions of adjustment.

There are at least two other possible reasons for the conflicting findings: use of different measures of adjustment and cultural factors. That is, the different findings may mean that results are restricted to a considerable extent to the particular measures used, and/or that there is a cross-cultural difference between American and Australian children with respect to the nature of their adjustment.

The most reasonable general conclusion at the present time seems to be that all-embracing generalisations about child adjustment are unlikely to have general validity. Discussions of "the whole personality in its total environment" (Wright,[1] p. 43) are likely to be meaningless unless precise statements are made about both the populations studied and the measures used.

It follows from these arguments that the findings discussed in this paper cannot be used to provide definitive answers to the sociological evaluations of American education which were presented earlier. It is possible, however, to consider at least two implications which the Melbourne findings appear to have for Australian education. These implications would be worth serious consideration if the Melbourne findings were confirmed on another carefully defined and fairly representative population of Australian primary school children, especially if some different measures were used.

The first implication is that, at least with respect to most ten- to eleven-year-old boys from intact, urban families, there seems ample reason to query the rather sweeping generalisation (Oeser[26]) that "poor learners in a classroom are also poor in satisfactory relations with others in a class . . . and when their peer relations are adjusted, their learning also improves". While the Melbourne study was not designed to provide a direct test of this assertion, the evidence presented here is certainly at variance with it.

Another implication of that study is that a moderate level of anxiety and the acquisition of stable work habits at home are associated with academic proficiency (Cox[27]). Other writers have placed similar emphasis upon the importance of stable work habits. Sanford *et al.*[28] reached quite similar conclusions some years ago, and William James[29] expressed similar sentiments much more picturesquely a long time before in his famous chapter on Habit: "As we become permanent drunkards by so many separate drinks, so we become saints in the moral, and authorities and experts in the practical and scientific spheres, by so many separate acts and hours of work."

References

[1] H. J. WRIGHT, "Anxiety and Mental Health in the School Child", *The Bulletin of the British Psychological Society*, 1960, **40**, 43.

[2] J. C. COLEMAN, *Abnormal Psychology and Modern Life,* Scott Foresman, Chicago, 1956, p. 15.

[3] C. R. ROGERS, *Client-Centered Therapy*, Houghton Mifflin, Boston, 1951, p. 510.

[4] B. SAPPENFIELD, *Personality Dynamics*, Knopf, New York, 1956, p. 24.

[5] R. LAPIERE, *The Freudian Ethic*, Duell, Sloan and Pearce, New York, 1959.

[6] D. RIESMAN with N. GLAZER and R. DENNEY, *The Lonely Crowd*, Yale University Press, New Haven, 1950.

[7] W. H. WHYTE, Jr., *The Organization Man*, Simon and Schuster, New York, 1956.

[8] H. BECKER and A. BOSKOFF, *Modern Sociological Theory*, Dryden, New York, 1957.

[9] B. F. SKINNER, "The Science of Learning and the Art of Teaching", *Harvard Educational Review*, 1954, **24**, 86-97.

[10] P. F. PIERCE (Ed.), *Source Materials of the Educational Program: A Grade Book of Living and Learning Experiences*, Public Schools Press, Chicago, 1957.

[11] P. H. BOWMAN, *Mobilizing Community Resources for Youth: Identification and Treatment of Maladjusted, Delinquent and Gifted Children*, University of Chicago Supplementary Educational Monograph, No. 85, 1956.

[12] M. BUSWELL, "The Relationship between the Social Structure of the Classroom and the Academic Success of the Pupils", *The Journal of Experimental Education*, 1953, **22**, pp. 37-52.

[13] J. J. KURTZ and E. J. SWENSON, "Factors Related to Overachievement and Underachievement in School", *School Review*, 1951, **59**, pp. 472-80.

[14] F. N. COX, "The Measurement and Analysis of Adjustment in Boys Attending Fifth Grade (Primary) School". Unpublished doctoral dissertation, University of Melbourne, 1961.

[15] D. G. Beswick, "Group Association and Popularity of Pre-adolescent Boys". Unpublished M. A. thesis, University of Melbourne, 1958.

[16] J. S. WESTERN, "Some Values of Pre-adolescent Boys". Unpublished M.A. thesis, University of Melbourne, 1958.

[17] P. G. HERBST, "Analysis and Measurement of a Situation: The Child in the Family", *Human Relations*, 1953, **6**, pp. 113-40.

[18] F. N. Cox and P. M. LEAPER, "Assessing Some Aspects of Parent-Child Relationship", *Child Development*, 1961, **32**, pp. 637-49.

[19] S. B. SARASON, K. S. DAVIDSON, F. F. LIGHTHALL, R. R. WAITE and B. K. RUEBUSH, *Anxiety in Elementary School Children*, John Wiley & Sons, New York, 1960.

[20] F. N. COX, "An Assessment of the Achievement Behaviour System in Children", *Child Development*, 1962, **33**, pp. 907-16.

[21] F. N. COX, "An Assessment of Children's Attitudes Towards Parent Figures", *Child Development*, 1962, **33**, pp. 821-30.

[22] H. A. MURRAY, *Explorations in Personality*, Oxford University Press, New York, 1938.

[23] D. G. BESWICK and F. N. COX, "Reputed Aggression and Dependence in Children", *Australian Journal of Psychology*, 1958, **10**, pp. 144-50.

24 W. GOLDFARB, "Psychological Privation in Infancy and Subsequent Adjustment", *American Journal of Orthopsychiatry*, 1945, **15**, pp. 247-55.

25 L. M. TERMAN and M. H. ODEN, *The Gifted Child Grows Up*, Stanford University Press, Stanford, 1947.

26 O. A. OESER (Ed.), *Teacher, Pupil and Task*, Tavistock, London, 1955.

27 F. N. COX, "Correlates of General and Test Anxiety in Children", *Australian Journal of Psychology*, 1960, **12**, pp. 169-77.

28 R. N. SANFORD, MARGARET M. ADKINS, R. B. MILLER and ELIZABETH COBB, "Physique, Personality and Scholarship", *Monograph for Social Research in Child Development*, 1943, **8**, No. 1.

29 W. JAMES, *The Principles of Psychology*, Vol. 1, Dover Publications Inc., New York, 1950, p. 127.

Chapter 11

The Relationship Between Personality and Achievement Variables in the Elementary School

ARNOLD H. MATLIN and
FRANCES A. MENDELSOHN
Hofstra University

Scores on the following variables were obtained for 68 fifth-grade students: IQ (Otis Quick Scoring Mental Abilities Test); school achievement (report card grades); standardised test achievement (Stanford Achievement Test); personal and social adjustment (California Test of Personality).

Zero-order and partial correlations indicated, as predicted, that personality adjustment is more strongly related to teachers' grades than to standardised achievement scores. This suggests that personality factors may be related to scholastic achievement because teachers tend to assign grades on the basis of adjustment as well as accomplishment, although other explanations are possible. The data also indicate that it is erroneous to assume that personal adjustment and social adjustment sections of the California Test of Personality are truly measuring different aspects of adjustment.

The importance of non-intellectual factors in academic achievement has long been discussed. One such factor often linked with scholastic achievement is personality adjustment. Researchers have pointed out

The authors wish to acknowledge the kind assistance of Mr. H. Barber, Principal, Walnut Street School, Uniondale, New York; Dr. J. P. Mooney, Assistant Superintendent, Uniondale School District; Dr. Anne Morgenstern, Division of Education, Hofstra University; and Dr. Julia Vane, Department of Psychology, Hofstra University, Hempstead, New York.

From the *Journal of Educational Research*, 1965, **58**, No. 10, pp. 457-59. Reprinted by permission of Arnold H. Matlin, Frances A. Mendelsohn and Dembar Educational Research Services.

a definite relationship between personality factors and scholastic achievement. For a partial review of this research, see Tyler[1] (pp. 123-29).

Unfortunately, relatively few studies have been concerned with the effect of personality factors at the elementary school level. Several studies which deal with the problem have been carried out (Tyler,[1] Abrams,[2] d'Heurle *et al*,[3] Liebman,[4] Norman and Daley,[5] Semler,[6] Wilson[7]). In general, with the exception of Wilson, the findings were that there exists a significant difference in the degree of academic achievement between groups of well adjusted and poorly adjusted elementary school children. More specifically, achieving students had a more adequate level of both personal and social adjustment than did underachieving students. It was the major purpose of the present study to further investigate the relationship between school achievement and the emotional and social adjustment of the elementary school child.

Inherent in the educational system is the fact that there exists a great deal of personal interaction between teacher and elementary school pupils. It seems reasonable to assume that the teacher when assigning grades will be influenced, consciously or unconsciously, by the student's personality adjustment as evidenced by his classroom behaviour. Conversely, standard achievement tests are constructed, administered, and scored impersonally. Therefore we would expect these scores to be less affected by personality adjustment variables.

On the basis of these considerations and the results of cited studies, it was predicted that adjustment, as measured by the California Test of Personality (CTP) would be positively correlated with achievement. However, it was predicted that adjustment would correlate more highly with teachers' grades than with scores on standard achievement tests.

Procedure

Ss were 68 children from three fifth grade classes in a predominantly middle class school district. For each subject, information was obtained on five variables. Measures of intelligence were obtained from scores on the Otis Quick Scoring Mental Abilities Test. Achievement on standardised tests was obtained from the battery median of the Stanford Achievement Tests. Classroom achievement was obtained by averaging report card grades over three marking periods. The California Test of Personality, Elementary Level (Form AA), was administered, and scores on the personal and social adjustment sections were obtained.

Results

The intercorrelation matrix for all variables is presented in Table 11.1

Inspection of the matrix reveals that achievement, as measured by teachers' ratings, has a 0·44 and a 0·42 correlation with personal and social adjustment respectively. Achievement as measured by standardised tests, however, has only a 0·30 and a 0·26 correlation with personal and social adjustment.

TABLE 11.1

Correlation Between All Variables

(N—68)

	IQ	Achievement (teachers' grades)	Achievement (Test)	Personal adjustment	Social adjustment
IQ	—	0·60 * * *	0·59 * * *	0·33 * * *	0·32 * * *
Achievement (teachers' grades)		—	0·73 * * *	0·44 * * *	0·42 * * *
Achievement (test)			—	0·30 * *	0·26 *
Personal adjustment				—	0·68 * * *
Social adjustment					—

* Significant beyond 0·05 level of confidence.
* * Significant beyond 0·02 level of confidence.
* * * Significant beyond 0·01 level of confidence.

IQ correlates with both achievement and adjustment. Thus, in order to determine the relationship between adjustment and achievement when the IQ variable was controlled, first-order partial correlations were computed and are presented in Table 11.2. These correlations enable us to assess the relationship between factors, with the variance due to IQ differences held constant. First-order correlations with IQ partialled out yielded significant 0·32 and 0·30 correlations between teachers' rating of student achievement and personal and social adjustment respectively. However, between achievement as measured by standardisd tests, and personal and social adjustment, the partial correlations are only 0·09 and 0·14.

TABLE 11.2

First-order Partial Correlations Between Achievement and Adjustment with IQ Held Constant

	Achievement (test)	Achievement (teachers' grades)
Personal adjustment	0·14	0·32 * * *
Social adjustment	0·09	0·30 * *

* * Significant beyond the 0·02 level of confidence.
* * * Significant beyond the 0·01 level of confidence.

A high correlation, 0·68, may be noted between personal and social adjustment sections of the CTP. Also notable is the similarity of correlations between the two adjustment sections and all other variables.

Discussion

As was expected, high correlations were found between IQ scores and both measures of achievement. As predicted, however, adjustment factors also contribute their share to the variance. Once IQ is partialled out, adjustment factors are still significantly related to school grades, but show little relation to scores on standard achievement tests. This finding confirms the prediction that adjustment correlates with achievement, but more strongly so in the case of report card grades than standardised achievement tests. The data suggest that adjustment may not be affecting achievement, *per se*. Rather, adjustment may actually affect the teacher's perception of the child's achievement. In other words, well adjusted and poorly adjusted pupils may perform equally well, but teachers may give better grades to the better adjusted students. However, alternative hypotheses can be formulated. Students with poor adjustment may have work habits and lack of persistence which could affect their achievement as evidenced by report card grades, whereas such variables may not affect scores on standard achievement tests.

The high r ($0 \cdot 68$) between the personal and social adjustment sections of the CTP, and the fact that the correlations of these sections with other variables are almost identical, indicated that it is probably erroneous to assume that the two subtests are truly measuring different aspects of adjustment. Future researchers and users of the test would probably be better advised to combine the sections into one general adjustment scale.

Summary

Data concerning IQ, school achievement, standardised test achievement and personality adjustment were obtained for 68 fifth grade pupils. As predicted, adjustment was strongly related to teachers' grades, but not to scores on the standardised test. It is concluded that personality variables may indirectly affect school grades at this level because teachers tend to base their grades on adjustment as well as accomplishment.

References

[1] L. S. TYLER, *The Psychology of Human Differences* (2nd Ed.), Appleton-Century-Crofts, New York, 1956.

[2] J. C. ABRAMS, "A Study of Certain Personality Characteristics of Non-Readers and Achieving Readers", *Dissertation Abstracts*, 1956, **16**, pp. 377-78.

[3] A. D'HEURLE, J. C. MELLINGER, and E. A. HAGGARD, "Personality, Intellectual and Achievement Patterns in Gifted Children", *Psychological Monographs*, 1959, **73**, 13, No. 4837.

[4] O. B. LEIBMAN, "The Relationship of Personal and Social Adjustment to Academic Achievement in the Elementary School", *Dissertation Abstracts*, **14**, 1954, p. 67.

[5] R. D. NORMAN and M. F. DALEY, "The Comparative Personality Adjustment of Superior and Inferior Readers", *Journal of Educational Psychology*, 1959, **50**, pp. 32-36.

[6] I. J. SEMLER, "Relationships Among Several Measures of Pupil Adjustment", *Journal of Educational Psychology*, 1960, **51**, pp. 60-64.

[7] J. A. R. WILSON, "Achievement, Intelligence, Age and Promotion Characteristics of Students Scoring at or below the Tenth Percentile on the California Test of Personality", *Journal of Educational Research*, 1959, **52**, pp. 283-92.

Chapter 12

The Relationship of Adjustment, Anxiety and Intelligence to Mathematics Performance

FRANK D. NAYLOR and ERIC GAUDRY
University of Melbourne

Can a non-normative measure of adjustment account for performance in mathematics independently of anxiety or intelligence? The mathematics performance of 621 Grade 7 children was analysed in relation to a measure of adjustment derived from semantic differential responses to "Myself" and "The Person I Would Like To Be". Covariance analyses for trait-anxiety, test-anxiety, and intelligence were carried out. It was found that the measure of adjustment was significantly related to mathematics performance after the effects of anxiety and intelligence were partialled out.

This report is derived from a larger study of the evaluative connotations of school children's personal and educational concepts. It concerns a non-normative operational definition of adjustment, and whether it can account for performance in mathematics independently of intelligence and anxiety.

The confused nature of the notion of adjustment is reflected in differing and sometimes contradictory results concerning the relation between adjustment variables and scholastic achievement. In its derivation from psychotherapy it frequently possesses honorific connotations, suggesting end-points or criteria whereby a person will be or become "fully functioning" (Rogers[1]). Adjustment is thereby assumed to be a unitary phenomenon whose effects permeate every aspect of be-haviour. In a scholastic context, however, such effects are far from

From the *Journal of Educational Research* (in press).
Reprinted by permission of Frank D. Naylor, Eric Gaudry and Dembar Educational Research Services.

being unequivocally documented. Cox[2] reported that in fifth grade Australian boys academic and social adjustment were quite independent of one another. This finding led him to argue that a concept of global adjustment stimulated sweeping generalisations concerning its effects in education, which were not in accordance with the evidence. Ringness[3] reported no gross adjustment differences between academically successful and non-successful Ss, although there were trends in his results which suggested slight differences. Matlin and Mendelsohn[4] found positive correlations between measures of social and personal adjustment and achievement, as indicated by grades given by teachers and objective test results. However, when IQ was partialled out of these correlations no relationship remained between adjustment and objective test results. A positive correlation between adjustment and grades given by teachers still remained. The authors suggested that teachers may give better grades to the better adjusted students even though their actual performance was no better than that of poorly adjusted students.

Positive correlations between various measures of self-concept and school performance have also been reported. Bruck and Bodwin[5] found a positive correlation between a projective measure of self-concept and the presence or absence of underachievement, which suggested that the relationship was worthy of detailed exploration. Jones and Strowig[6] found a positive correlation between self-concept of ability assessed by items on a Guttman-type scale, and performance. This measure was as effective a predictor of performance as an ability measure. Their self-concept measure was based on the assumption that individuals are capable of accurate self-report regarding feelings about themselves. This assumption underlies a great deal of research using self-concept measures. The evaluation of client-centred therapy (Rogers and Dymond[7]) and career development (Super[8]) have used self-report measures of varying degrees of directness, but their validity has had to be assumed.

Two main issues arise from these considerations. The first concerns definitions of adjustment. The normative connotations of the concept can be seen in the way in which it is indexed by particular responses to anxiety scales and personality inventories. In such devices the problems of faking and response sets are well known (Edwards[9]), and in so far as an individual is impressed by normative notions of adjustment the temptation, and perhaps the necessity, to distort responses in order to project a favourable image is understandable. The criteria of adjustment in this sense are thus imposed in terms of value judgements concerning appropriate ways of behaving and feeling. It would seem possible, however, to achieve a more relative concept of adjustment than this, and Rogers[10] has attempted this in his theories of client-centred therapy. Adjustment is regarded by Rogers[10] as "congruence" between self and experience, implying non-normative definitions since the individual's self and his experiences are unique to himself. Dymond[11] used the Q-sort (Stephenson[12]) statements developed by Butler and Haigh[13] to obtain an index of personal adjustment as a consequence of therapy, but an *a priori* determination of the kinds of responses which indicated good adjustment was made. Crowne, Stephens and Kelly[14] found that the tendency to give socially desirable responses was negatively correlated with the discrepancy between self and ideal-self on a Q-sort, indicating that the Q-sort technique was also susceptible to the influence of social desirability response sets.

The second issue concerns the problem of achieving an operational definition of adjustment. In so far as the term possesses normative connotations, such that it is implicitly clear to the respondent how a well adjusted person would respond, then responses are going to be confounded with social desirability. If Rogers' theory concerning the outcomes of therapy is correct it would seem to require a definition of congruence in non-normative terms, and its operational index should be similarly non-normative. An approach to such a definition seems possible in terms of the meaning of self and ideal-self concepts to the individual. The relation between such meanings appears to meet all the requirements of Rogers' qualitative definition of congruence[10] without the normative connotations which stimulate socially desirable responses, and with the minimal imposition of a frame of reference for responding.

The semantic differential technique (Osgood, Suci and Tannenbaum[15]) has been developed to measure connotative meaning, and it possesses certain qualities which might enable it to be used as an operational definition of adjustment without the shortcomings referred to above. In this technique similarity in the meaning of concepts is indexed by D scores.[15] These scores index the qualitative similarity of concepts within but not between individuals. The similarity in meaning of the concepts "myself" and "the person I would like to be" (M-I) is defined by the individual.

This similarity in meaning need have no qualitative similarity with the definitions of other individuals, and yet may be quantitatively similar. Thus one individual could rate both self and ideal self as "good", while another could rate them both as "bad". The qualitative differences in the ratings between the individuals are quite manifest, but in so far as the meaning of the concepts—as "good" or "bad"— is identical within each individual the quantitative index (the D scores) for both individuals will have the same value. Whether or not, from some external standpoint, a person rates himself "favourably" or "unfavourably" does not influence the quantitative statement of the relation between the meanings of different concepts which the D scores express. On this account the semantic differential technique can be taken to be non-normative in its index of the similarity of the meaning of different concepts to an individual. The D scores for M-I can therefore stand as an operational definition of adjustment without the normative connotations implied by value-oriented judgements of "good" and "poor" adjustment.

Measures of anxiety were included in this study because various indicators of anxiety level have frequently been taken as an operational definition of adjustment (Brackbill and Little,[16] Cox[2]). That is, a high level of anxiety has been equated with poor adjustment. The use of an anxiety measure as an index of adjustment is complicated by the fact that at least one anxiety measure, the Achievement Anxiety Test (Alpert and Haber[17]) contains two scales, a nine-item "facilitating" anxiety scale and a ten-item "debilitating" anxiety scale. The authors, Alpert and Haber, maintain that "an individual may possess a large amount of both anxieties, or of one but not the other, or none of either".

A further complication is added by the distinction made by Spielberger[18, 19] between trait and state anxiety. State-anxiety (*A*-State) is conceptualised as "a transitory emotional state or condition of the organism that is characterised by subjective, consciously perceived feelings of tension and apprehension and heightened autonomic nervous system activity. State-anxiety may vary in intensity and fluctuate over time."

Trait-anxiety (*A*-Trait) refers to relatively stable individual differences in anxiety proneness, that is, to differences between people in the tendency to respond to situations perceived as threatening with elevations in *A*-State intensity.

In general, it would be expected that those who are high in *A*-Trait will exhibit *A*-State elevations more frequently than low *A*-Trait individuals because they tend to perceive a wider range of situations as dangerous or threatening. High *A*-Trait persons are also more likely to respond to stressful situations with increased *A*-State intensity, especially in situations that involve interpersonal relationships which pose some threat to self-esteem.

Trait-anxiety, therefore, is generic while state-anxiety measures a specific anxiety aroused in a particular situation. The Test Anxiety Scale for Children or TASC (Sarason *et al.*[20]) is more specific than Spielberger's *A*-Trait scale in that it is assumed to measure anxiety reactions to test and test-like situations in the school setting. However, it is less specific than the *A*-State scale in that it is concerned with a whole range of test situations whereas the state scale can be framed to get at a particular response by changing the stem question. For example, if an investigation was concerned with anxiety about making a speech the question might be, "How did you feel as you rose to your feet to begin your speech?"

Even if it is possible to distinguish between these types of anxiety, to take scores on any one of the three as an operational index of adjustment ignores possible facilitating effects. This is not to argue that anxiety and adjustment are independent, but merely that anxiety cannot be held to be an inevitable predicate of poor adjustment. Anxiety and adjustment may therefore be distinct constructs which become related under particular conditions. What these conditions are may vary between individuals and on this account a particular individual's anxiety level does not necessarily have implications for his adjustment. The semantic differential measure can be regarded as a measure of adjustment quite distinct from the scales which measure the anxiety constructs. Whether or not the *D* scores on the *SD* are actually independent of the anxiety measures is therefore one of the central empirical questions of this study.

Intelligence test score has been shown to account for a significant percentage of the variance of measures of academic performance. Matlin and Mendelsohn[4] showed that the amount of variance in objective test performance in school subjects accounted for by adjustment measures was also accounted for by individual differences in intelligence. A further empirical question in this study, therefore, is whether intelligence can account for the effects of adjustment in mathematics performance.

Method

Subjects. The Ss were 316 male and 305 female Grade 7 children enrolled in 18 classes at different schools in Melbourne, Australia. These schools represented a cross-section of the various types of secondary schools in the city, in that government and non-government, single-sex and co-educational schools were in the sample.

Instruments. The Test Anxiety Scale for Children or TASC (Sarason et al.[20]) slightly modified to make it suitable for Australian conditions, an intelligence test of the Otis type, and the State-Trait Anxiety Inventory or STAI (Spielberger, Gorsuch and Lushene[21]) were administered. The specific statement used in the State form of the STAI was "Indicate how you feel when you are doing an important mathematics test".

A semantic differential was also completed by the Ss. This consisted of 11 different concepts each judged on 18 bipolar adjectival scales. The concepts, which were presented in counterbalanced orders to minimise sequence effects, were: (1) myself, (2) my mother, (3) my father, (4) school pupils, (5) school teachers, (6) top of the class, (7) the person I would like to be, (8) pleasant and good things, (9) unpleasant and bad things, (10) school, and (11) examinations.

The 18 scales were: sweet-sour, glad-sad, fast-slow, wet-dry, hard-soft, weak-strong, tall-small, good-bad, thick-thin, long-short, first-last, before-behind, inside-outside, light-dark, active-passive, below-above, warm-cool, and poor-rich.

Mathematics marks were obtained from the school records of the Ss' performance on the mid-year examinations.

Procedure. The intelligence test, the anxiety scales, and the semantic differential were administered several weeks before the mid-year examination.

Mathematics marks within each class were converted to T scores with a mean of 50 and a standard deviation of 10 to make the marks comparable across classes.

The semantic differential was factor-analysed to isolate those scales which clearly defined an Evaluative factor. These scales were: sweet-sour, glad-sad, fast-slow, good-bad, first-last, before-behind, and active-passive. In his review of the generality of affective meaning systems, Osgood[22] reported that an Evaluation factor was the most reliable one to emerge from studies of connotative meaning. The first factor in the present factor analysis was defined by the scales referred to above.

D scores (Osgood, Suci and Tannenbaum[15]) of profile congruence on the Evaluative factor for *M-I* were calculated, and two groups were formed by splitting these scores at the median. Where reference is made to these two groups in the subsequent text, the word "Near" is used to describe the group whose *D* scores were small and whose *M-I* profiles were relatively close. The word "Far" is used to describe the other half. The *A*-State scores were also split at the median to form high- and low-anxious groups.

Results

The data were analysed by a multivariate analysis of variance in a $2 \times 2 \times 2$ design. Within each class there were two levels of sex, two levels of *D* scores on the *M-I* profiles and two levels of state-anxiety. The dependent variables were intelligence, trait-anxiety, TASC and mathematics scores. There were no significant interactions but the multivariate contrast for all three main effects was significant at the 0·001 level. Table 12.1 shows the results of the univariate *F* tests for Sex, *M-I*, and *A*-State. The mean mathematics scores for the significant results for Table 12.1 are shown in column 1 of Table 12.3.

TABLE 12.1
Univariate *F* Tests for Sex, *M-I* and *A*-State
(*df* 1, 613)

Variable	Sex		*M-I*		*A*-State	
	F	*p*	*F*	*p*	*F*	*p*
Otis	0·03	0·869	16·04	0·001	8·20	0·004
A-Trait	0·16	0·693	15·67	0·001	78·44	0·001
TASC	28·22	0·001	30·75	0·001	128·25	0·001
Maths	0·28	0·594	13·99	0·001	4·29	0·035

The relationship between the independent variables and performance in mathematics was the focal point of the investigation. The significant differences listed in Table 12.1 made it essential to carry out covariance analyses to discover whether the significant effects would be maintained. Using mathematics marks as the sole dependent variable, the data were re-analysed first with intelligence as the covariate, then with the trait anxiety as the covariate, and finally with TASC as the covariate. The significant *A*-State and Sex differences reported in Table 12.1 were not maintained but the *M-I* comparisons were. Table 12.2 contains a summary of the results for the *M-I* comparison.

TABLE 12.2
Mean Mathematics Scores for the *M-I* Comparison
Adjusted for Three Covariates (*df* 1, 612)

Covariate	*F*	*p*	Adjusted Means	
			Far *M-I*	Near *M-I*
Otis	4·06	0·044	49·52	50·91
A-Trait	10·42	0·001	48·97	51·50
TASC	7·06	0·008	49·19	51·27

In Table 12.3, the unadjusted mathematics means for the significant main effects referred to in Table 12.1 are given in column 1. The adjusted means for the covariance analyses are presented in columns 2, 3 and 4.

TABLE 12.3

Unadjusted and Adjusted Mathematics Mean Scores for Sex, *M-I* and State Anxiety

Factor		Unadjusted means	Intelligence	Means adjusted for A-Trait	TASC
Sex	Male	50·40	50·43	50·39	50·01
	Female	50·00	49·96	50·01	50·40
M-I	Far	48·78	49·52	48·97	49·19
	Near	51·70	50·91	51·50	51·27
A-State	High	49·17	49·83	49·62	50·06
	Low	51·29	50·59	50·82	50·35

Discussion

The most important results from a theoretical point of view were the maintenance of the three significant comparisons shown in Table 12.2. While the significant differences in mathematics performance between the high and low *A*-State groups were taken out by all covariance adjustments, the significant differences in mathematics performance of the Far and Near *M-I* groups were maintained. The effect of each covariance adjustment (Table 12.3) brought the mean scores of both groups closer together but the change was so small that the significant *M-I* comparisons remained.

These results differ from those obtained by Matlin and Meldelsohn,[4] Ringness[3] and are compatible with those of Jones and Strowig.[6] In the Matlin and Mendelsohn[4] study, the significant correlations between adjustment and performance became non-significant when the effect of intelligence was partialled out. In the present study the covariance adjustment for intelligence brought the mean mathematics scores closer together but a significant "adjustment effect" remained. Unlike Ringness' results, the present results show unequivocal adjustment differences.

Cox[2] argued that a concept of global adjustment was too all-embracing to account for the particular findings in his study. However, his criteria of adjustment were implicitly normative and thus were subject to social desirability response sets. Since the norms of the classroom and those of the peer group and family need not be similar to one another, the different connotations of social desirability in these contexts could have led to differential responding depending on the situation. The concept of global adjustment as used by Rogers,[10] is context-free. The acceptance of the Rogerian framework requires the use of non-normative and thereby context-free measures. The rejection of this notion of global adjustment cannot be validly achieved through the use of normative measures.

In the present study, the effects of adjustment, as defined by the *D* scores for *M-I*, are not accounted for by individual differences in intelligence. The relationship between adjustment and performance in mathematics after the covariance analyses is strong enough to suggest that intelligence and adjustment are quite distinct constructs.

The use of anxiety measures as an operational definition of adjustment is based on the assumption that poor adjustment logically entails anxiety. The present results show that this is not the case. The effects of general anxiety level (A-Trait) and of test anxiety (TASC) do not account for the effects of adjustment when they are used as covariates. If there was a necessary relation between anxiety and adjustment such that poor adjustment was inevitably associated with high anxiety then this result would not have been obtained. Adjustment is thereby a construct distinct from A-Trait and TASC.

The relationship between A-State and adjustment was not entirely clear in these findings. There was no interaction between A-State and adjustment but they did have independent effects on unadjusted mathematics performance. However, all the covariance adjustments accounted for the difference in performance due to A-State whereas none of them accounted for the differences due to adjustment. The implications of this finding are being investigated in the larger study. Clearly the semantic differential can be used as a non-normative operational definition of adjustment unconfounded by the effects of normative measures of anxiety and intelligence.

References

[1] C. R. ROGERS, "A Theory of Therapy, Personality, and Interpersonal Relationships, as Developed in the Client-Centered Framework", in S. Koch (Ed.), *Psychology: a Study of a Science, Vol. 3: Formulations of the Person and the Social Context*, McGraw-Hill, New York, 1959.

[2] F. N. Cox, "Academic and Social Adjustment in 5th grade Boys", *Australian Journal of Education*, 1961, 5, pp. 185-92.

[3] T. A. RINGNESS, "The Emotional Adjustment of Academically Successful and Nonsuccessful Bright Ninth Grade Boys". *Journal of Educational Research*, 1965, 59, pp. 88-91.

[4] A. H. MATLIN and F. A. MENDELSOHN, "The Relationship between Personality and Achievement Variables in the Elementary School", *Journal of Educational Research*, 1965, 58, pp. 457-59.

[5] M. BRUCK and R. F. BODWIN, "The Relationship between Self-Concept and the Presence and Absence of Scholastic Underachievement", *Journal of Clinical Psychology*, 1962, 18, pp. 181-82.

[6] J. G. JONES and R. W. STROWIG, "Adolescent Identity and Self-Perception as Predictors of Scholastic Achievement", *Journal of Educational Research*, 1968, 62, pp. 78-81.

[7] C. R. ROGERS and ROSALIND F. DYMOND (Eds), *Psychotherapy and Personality Change*, University of Chicago Press, Chicago, 1954.

[8] D. E. SUPER, "The Definition and Measurement of Early Career Behavior: A First Formulation". *Personnel and Guidance Journal*, 1963, 41, pp. 775-80.

[9] A. L. EDWARDS, *The Social Desirability Variable in Personality Assessment and Research*, Dryden, New York, 1957.

[10] C. R. ROGERS, *On Becoming a Person*, Houghton Mifflin, Boston, 191.

11 ROSALIND F. DYMOND, "Adjustment Changes over Therapy for Self-Sorts", in C. R. Rogers and Rosalind F. Dymond (Eds), *Psychotherapy and Personality Change*, University of Chicago Press, Chicago, 1954.

12 W. STEPHENSON, *The Study of Behavior, Q-Technique and its Methodology*, University of Chicago Press, Chicago, 1963.

13 J. M. BUTLER and G. V. HAIGH, "Changes in the Relation between Self-Concepts and Ideal Concepts Consequent upon Client-Centered Counseling", in C. R. Rogers and Rosalind F. Dymond (Eds), *Psychotherapy and Personality Change*, University of Chicago Press, Chicago, 1954.

14 D. P. CROWNE, M. W. STEPHENS and R. KELLY, "The Validity and Equivalence of Tests of Self-Acceptance", *Journal of Psychology*, 1961, **51**, pp. 101-12.

15 C. E. OSGOOD, G. SUCI and P. TANNENBAUM, *The Measurement of Meaning*, University of Illinois Press, Urbana, 1957.

16 G. BRACKBILL, and K. B. LITTLE, "MMPI Correlates of the Taylor Scale of Manifest Anxiety", *Journal of Consulting Psychology*, 1954, **18**, pp. 433-36.

17 R. ALPERT and R. N. HABER, "Anxiety in Academic Achievement Situations", *Journal of Abnormal and Social Psychology*, 1960, **68**, pp. 207-15.

18 C. D. SPIELBERGER, "Theory and Research on Anxiety", in C. D. Spielberger (Ed.), *Anxiety and Behavior*, Academic Press, New York, 1966.

19 E. GAUDRY and C. D. SPIELBERGER, *Anxiety and Educational Achievement*, John Wiley & Sons, Sydney, 1971.

20 S. B. SARASON, K. S. DAVIDSON, F. F. LIGHTHALL, R. S. WAITE and B. K. RUEBUSH, *Anxiety in Elementary School Children*, John Wiley & Sons, New York, 1960.

21 C. D. SPIELBERGER, R. L. GORSUCH and R. E. LUSHENE, *The State-Trait Anxiety Inventory (STAI), Test Manual for Form X*, Consulting Psychologists Press, Palo Alto, 1970.

22 C. E. OSGOOD, "Studies of the Generality of Affective Meaning Systems", *American Psychologist*, 1962, **17**, pp. 10-28.

Chapter 13

The Self Concept of High, Medium and Low Academic Achievers

A. E. EVERETT
University of Newcastle

The importance of the self concept in personality and educational research has been recognised for a considerable period. Lecky[1] was one of the earlier workers who suggested that scholastic performance tended to be consistent with the individual's self-assessment. The same theme has been developed in the clinical setting by Rogers;[2] optimal psychological adjustment involves a high degree of congruence between the conceptual and behavioural components of the individual's life space.

Despite the large volume of literature generated by research on the self concept, there is still not available any widely accepted precise statement of the personality differences between high and low achievers. One of the few reviews in this area (Taylor[3]) indicates that high achievers tend to have positive self values and interpersonal relationships; they have realistic goal orientations, accept authority, manifest directed (rather than free-floating) academic anxiety, have academically (rather than socially) oriented activity patterns, and in general show low conflict in the independence-dependence area. Low achievers are characterised by the opposite polar traits. Holland and Nichols[4] found that the best predictors at college level consisted of two types of measures: one based on actual high school achievement, the second a composite measure based on goals, interests and self concept measures.

A further general finding (Bendig,[5] Haun[6]) is that introversion and academic achievement are positively related. However, the relationships are usually too low to be of predictive value. In spite of the above-mentioned research consensus, many conflicting findings are available;

From the *Australian Journal of Education*, 1971, **15**, No. 3, pp. 319-24. Reprinted by permission of A. V. Everett and the Australian Council for Educational Research.

Combs *et al.*[7] suggest that "no area of psychological research is currently more popular or more confused than that having to do with the measurement of the self concept" (p. 493). Likewise Wallace[8] suggests that the theoretical conceptions have outstripped the measuring tools.

The measuring instruments available include self-report inventories, *Q*-sorts, projective techniques, and the semantic differential (Osgood *et al.*[9]). A modified form of the semantic differential (*SD*) was used in the present study. Due to the lack of unambiguous research findings in this area, the aim was to provide a qualitative and descriptive picture of the self concept configurations of high, medium, and low academic achievers.

Method and Results

The sample consisted of 59 female students in a Catholic residential college at the University of Queensland in 1966. Each subject completed an *SD* assessment of 26 concepts on nine bipolar scales. The concepts were selected in a pilot study involving an independent sample of 32 subjects. They were asked to nominate any concepts they considered important in student life. This data was tabulated in the form of a frequency distribution and the 26 most frequently nominated concepts were chosen for use in the major study. These 26 concepts are listed in Fig. 13.1, and tend to fall into a number of categories: concepts involving the self (1-2), achievement-related concepts (3-9), student activities (10-14), institutional concepts (15-17), a social activity group of concepts (18-23) and clinical concepts (24-26). The nine bipolar scales were arbitrarily selected from the *SD* literature. They were fast-slow, irresponsible-responsible, exciting-unexciting, light-heavy, tense-relaxed, foolish-wise, mature-immature, cold-hot and hard-soft.

The independent variable of academic achievement was measured by means of a Grade Point Average (GPA) based on yearly examination results obtained by subjects subsequent to the collection of the *SD* data. A number of points was allocated for the grade obtained in each course attempted, ranging from zero for a failure to six for a maximum pass. These points were then added for each subject and divided by the number of courses attempted. On the assumption that the personality differences between achievement levels would be most marked in the extremes, the distribution of the GPA was examined and three criterion groups of high, medium and low academic achievers were selected; each achievement level contained nine subjects.

In each of the three criterion groups the sum of the nine Ss on the 26 concepts for each of the nine scales was calculated and each of the three resulting 26×9 (concepts by scales) matrices were put through a hierarchical classification programme, "Class", discussed by Lance and Williams.[10]*

The classification of the 26 concepts in nine dimensions (scales) results in concepts with the greatest profile similarity on the nine scales

*The CD 3600 computer at the Computing Research Section in Canberra was used.

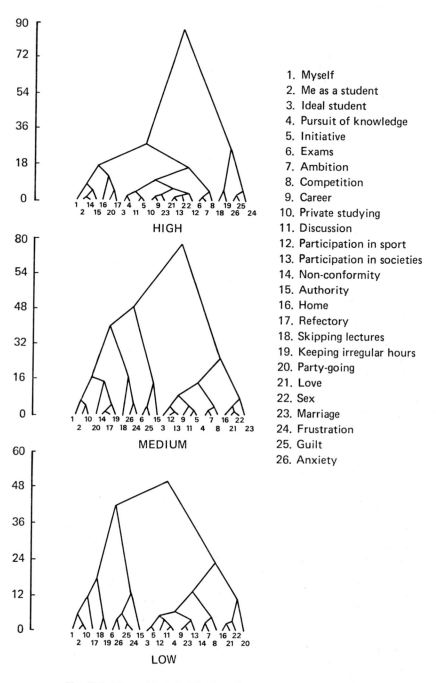

1. Myself
2. Me as a student
3. Ideal student
4. Pursuit of knowledge
5. Initiative
6. Exams
7. Ambition
8. Competition
9. Career
10. Private studying
11. Discussion
12. Participation in sport
13. Participation in societies
14. Non-conformity
15. Authority
16. Home
17. Refectory
18. Skipping lectures
19. Keeping irregular hours
20. Party-going
21. Love
22. Sex
23. Marriage
24. Frustration
25. Guilt
26. Anxiety

Fig. 13.1 Hierarchical classification of concepts in high, medium, and low achieving groups. Ordinate axes represent square Euclidean distance between centroids of concept clusters.

being fused, the centroid of the fused concepts being recalculated and the classification proceeding until all the initial 26 concepts are fused in the final hierarchical plot. This hierarchical plot, output by the computer for each of the three achievement levels, with the list of the concepts and their identifying numbers is presented in Fig. 13.1. The ordinate axis gives the squared Euclidean distance between group centroids at various stages of the classification process.

Discussion

The first point that can be made is that meaningful and consistent differences do exist between the self concept configurations of high, medium, and low academic achievers. In the high achieving group the concepts most remote from the self concept cluster include the clinical concepts, frustration, guilt and anxiety, and also the non-achievement related social activity concepts, keeping irregular hours, and skipping lectures. In marked contrast, the medium and low achieving groups locate the concepts sex, love, and home most remotely from the self cluster together with the additional concepts marriage and party-going respectively.

At the other end of the spectrum the concepts most similar to self in the high achievers are non-conformity and authority, whilst the medium and low groups locate private studying with the self cluster. The low achievers rate the self cluster as being quite near the concepts refectory, skipping lectures and keeping irregular hours; the medium achievers see the self cluster as being in proximity to party-going, non-conformity, refectory and keeping irregular hours.

There is basic consensus in the three achievement groups with respect to the qualities of the ideal student; she is involved in discussion, the pursuit of knowledge, possesses initiative and participates in student activities. The major difference, however, is that in the high achieving group the ideal student is incorporated into the self cluster much earlier in the classification procedure than in the low or medium group.

Further meaningful differences emerge in the three groups with respect to the concept exams. In the medium group, exams is associated with guilt and authority and in the low group with the clinical concepts anxiety, guilt and frustration. In the high group, however, exams is linked with ambition and competition.

At a more molar level it can be seen from the ordinate values of square Euclidean distance between concept clusters that the degree of differentiation between concept clusters is positively related to achievement level. However, with the high achievers this differentiation is attributable to specific concepts, namely the clinical cluster, skipping lectures, and keeping irregular hours. All the remaining concepts are fused with the self cluster quite early in the classification. There is a high degree of similarity between the hierarchical plots of the medium and low achievers; at the stage where only two general clusters still exist the medium achievers include the concepts non-conformity and party-going with the self cluster, while the low achievers exclude these concepts from the self cluster. In contrast to the self cluster of the high achievers, that of the medium and low group contains a restricted number of concepts, that is, the self cluster of high achievers is a much more embracing and global configuration, which excludes only the clinical cluster and two non-achievement related concepts.

At this stage it is possible to present a descriptive statement of the self concept for each of the achievement levels. High achievers tend to perceive themselves as non-conformists and tend to accept authority; they see clinical concepts such as anxiety, frustration and guilt as being alien to their self concepts, and link such clinical concepts with non-achievement related activities such as keeping irregular hours and skipping lectures. Examinations they view in a context of competition and ambition. They do not see themselves as being far removed from the ideal student, and they participate in achievement-related endeavour (private study) which in turn is seen as a means to future-oriented activities such as career and marriage.

In contrast the average-achieving female student sees the self as being involved in private study and also in non-achievement activities like party-going and keeping irregular hours. They share with the high achievers the notion that they tend to be non-conformist. The medium achievers view exams in a context of guilt, anxiety, and frustration, in association with authority and skipping lectures. Unlike the high achievers, concepts of home, love, sex and marriage are quite alien to the self cluster while the clinical concepts form part of it.

The self concept of the low achiever is very similar to that of the medium achiever; however, the self is not seen as being non-conformist and party-going is quite remote from the self; exams and authority are enshrouded with connotations of anxiety, frustration and guilt; these clinical concepts in turn are linked with skipping lectures and keeping irregular hours and all of these concepts form part of the self cluster.

Some parallels between the present results and previous research are evident. The results are in accord with Taylor's findings that high achievers tend to accept authority; however, rather than exhibiting positive self values their self concepts are characterised by the absence of negative self values such as anxiety and guilt. The remoteness of these clinical concepts to the self concept provides relatively clear cut evidence of a relationship between academic achievement and perceived adjustment not readily available from other sources (Tyler,[11] p. 115). Anxiety in the high achiever was not found to be linked to academic situations (Taylor[3]), but nor was it found to be "free-floating"; rather it was meaningfully related to other clinical and non-achievement concepts and quite divorced from the self concept.

The present study, despite methodological differences from previous research does provide a qualitative and descriptive picture of the differences in the self concept configurations of high, medium and low achieving female college students. It is intended as an exploratory statement and is not concerned with the question of the significance of the differences discussed. Others (Marks and Murray[12]) have pointed to the inadequacy of the bivariate approach in an area such as this.

Hopefully the present study, employing existing multivariate computer techniques, will stimulate further research along these lines.

References

[1] P. LECKY, *Self-Consistency: A Theory of Personality,* Island Press, New York, 1945.

[2] C. R. ROGERS, *On Becoming a Person,* Houghton Mifflin, Boston, 1961.

[3] R. G. TAYLOR, "Personality Traits and Discrepant Achievement: A Review", *Journal of Counseling Psychology,* 1964, **11**, pp. 76-82.

[4] J. L. HOLLAND and R. C. NICHOLS, "Prediction of Academic and Extra-Curricular Achievement in College", *Journal of Educational Psychology,* 1964, **55**, pp. 55-65.

[5] A. W. BENDIG, "Extraversion, Neuroticism, and Student Achievement in Introductory Psychology", *Journal of Educational Research,* 1960, **53**, pp. 263-67.

[6] K. W. HAUN, "Note on Prediction of Academic Performance from Personality Test Scores", *Psychological Reports,* 1965, **16**, p. 294.

[7] A. W. COMBS, D. W. SOPER and C. C. COURSON, "The Measurement of Self Concept and Self Report". *Educational and Psychological Measurement,* 1963, **23**, pp. 493-500.

[8] J. G. WALLACE, *Concept Growth and the Education of the Child,* National Foundation for Educational Research in England and Wales, Occasional Publication Series No. 12, 1965.

[9] C. E. OSGOOD, G. J. SUCI, and P. H. TANNENBAUM, *The Measurement of Meaning,* University of Illinois Press, Urbana, 1957.

[10] G. N. LANCE and W. T. WILLIAMS, "A General Theory of Classificatory Sorting Strategies: I. Hierarchial Systems", *Computation Journal,* 1967, **9**, pp. 373-80.

[11] L. E. TYLER, *The Psychology of Human Differences,* Appleton-Century-Crofts, Meredith, New York, 1965.

[12] E. MARKS and J. E. MURRAY, "Nonadditive Effects in the Prediction of Academic Achievement", *Educational and Psychological Measurement,* 1965, **25**, pp. 1097-1104.

ACKNOWLEDGEMENT

The author is grateful to Dr. D. W. G. Timms for his guidance in the design of this study.

Chapter 14

Personality Factors and School Achievement: A Comparison of British and American Children

H. J. BUTCHER
Department of Education, University of Manchester

M. AINSWORTH
Sharston County Secondary School

J. E. NESBITT
Department of Education, University of Manchester

Samples of 12-14-year-old British and American children were tested with Cattell's HSPQ, and their mean scores compared on fourteen personality factors and two second-order factors (extraversion and anxiety). Significant differences were found on a number of factors and, in particular, the British children were found to be less sociable, more assertive and less conscientious. The pattern of prediction of school achievement was compared, and the same factors were in general found to be related to school achievement in both countries.

Introduction

Although it is widely recognised that personality factors play a part in determining school attainment, methods of assessing them have in general proved disappointing.

Middleton and Guthrie,[1] for example, say that "attempts to improve prediction by using non-intellective factors such as interests and personality traits have yielded quite discouraging results . . . the principal

From the *British Journal of Educational Psychology*, 1963, **33**, pp. 276-85. Reprinted by permission of H. J. Butcher and the *British-Journal of Educational Psychology*.

difficulty is probably heterogeneity of the criterion and non-summative or non-linear predictions".

It must be admitted that neither questionnaires nor objective tests of personality have yet reached the stage of acceptance as practical instruments of selection and guidance, while ratings are very often so bedevilled with halo effect as to be even less satisfactory. From the theoretical point of view, however, there are enough suggestive and interesting findings in the literature to make it clear that research is getting warm, so to speak, and that real effects are there to be discovered when the research instruments have been further standardised and refined. The High School Personality Questionnaire appears to be one of the more promising instruments available for use with children, and has the following advantages:

(*a*) It provides measures of fourteen primary factors, and also of two main second-order factors into which the primary factors fall, i.e. anxiety and extraversion.

(*b*) The factors measured have emerged from a considerable body of prolonged research. They are briefly described in the tables that follow. A full description is provided in the handbook of the test (Cattell, Beloff and Coan[2]).

(*c*) The factors correspond in most cases to those that have been extensively studied in adults.

(*d*) The test is designed to be used equally in the British and American cultures, and the items contain no glaring Americanisms or Anglicisms.

The present study is concerned with the following questions. Are there systematic differences between British and American children at age 12-14 on some or all of the fourteen primary and two main second-order factors which the HSPQ is designed to measure? What degree of prediction of school attainment is gained by the use of this test of personality? Do the same personality factors make for school success in England as in America?

Previous Research

CROSS-CULTURAL STUDIES OF PERSONALITY

Studies comparing British and American children in terms of personality factors appear to be scarce. Sarnoff *et al.*,[3] compared anxiety among American and English children (American from Connecticut, English from Hendon). They were primarily interested in validating a measure of test anxiety, and their hypothesis that English primary school children would show higher test anxiety than their opposite numbers in the U.S.A. was confirmed. On a test of general anxiety, however, no significant national difference was found.

Cattell and Warburton[4] compared the scores of American University students, British graduate students (student teachers) and British students at a College of Advanced Technology on the 16 PF test. On ten out of fifteen primary personality factors (excluding intelligence), differences were found between the American and British University students. In addition there were considerable differences between the two British samples (sometimes larger than the British-American differences) and these were statistically significant in the case of seven out of fifteen factors, with smaller groups being compared than in the case of the British-American comparisons. The groups were also compared in terms of the second-order factors of anxiety and extraversion and the British University students were found to be less anxious and more introverted than the American. British CAT students were least anxious and most extraverted of the three groups.

THE RELATION OF PERSONALITY FACTORS TO SCHOOL ATTAINMENT

Most studies have been concerned with the two broad factors of anxiety and extraversion-introversion. Findings have been rather conflicting, and the discrepancies can probably be assigned to some or all of the following causes:

(*a*) Differences in national culture pattern, e.g. extraversion may be more of an asset in American primary schools than in British;

(*b*) Different effects at different ages, e.g. it seems plausible, as suggested by Furneaux,[5] that introversion may be more of an asset at sixth-form and university level owing to changed conditions of work;

(*c*) Different definitions of the variables, and in particular a blurring of the distinction between anxiety and neuroticism. (A comparison, for instance, of anxiety scores based on the HSPQ and neuroticism scores based on the Maudsley personality inventory for children would be useful in this connection.)

(*d*) Non-linear relations between the variables, e.g. Cox's[6] finding that a middling degree of anxiety favoured school work, and Grooms and Endler's[7] that only with a high anxiety group did a test of personality yield any improvement in the prediction of achievement;

(*e*) Varying effects against different criteria, as in Lynn's[8] finding that anxiety had a different effect, according as the criterion was school work in English or in arithmetic;

(*f*) Sex differences. Women have been found to have higher average scores than men on introversion in a number of studies (e.g. Anderson[9]). It is also possible that the relation between introversion and school achievement shows a sex difference.

In view of these discrepancies, and of considerations of space, a systematic review of the literature will not be offered here. A useful survey of recent papers in this area is provided by Warburton.[10]

Method

SAMPLES USED

The American sample consisted of the entire seventh grade in two junior high schools in Springfield, Illinois and Paxton, Illinois. They were selected as representing contrasting types of area, Springfield being the state capital, with the school in question drawing almost exclusively on urban families, and Paxton being a small country town, to which many of the children came from the surrounding countryside. The numbers of children tested were 154 and 123, respectively. There were approximately equal numbers of boys and girls in each sample and the mean age was 12·7.

The first British sample consisted of all the first-year children in an eight-stream Secondary Modern school in South Manchester. The number of children tested was 230. There were 113 boys and 117 girls, and the mean age was 12·5.

The second British sample consisted of 140 children in the third year of secondary schooling. The mean age of the children at the time of testing was 14·3. The sample included equal numbers of boys and girls and was designed to be representative of the age-group in ability and of urban society in the socio-economic status of parents.

The availability of two separate samples from different schools in both the U.S.A. and in England provides useful evidence concerning intra-country as well as inter-country differences.

ADMINISTRATION OF THE TESTS

The three authors were responsible for administering the tests to the American samples, to the British Secondary Modern sample, and to the representative British sample respectively. At Springfield, Illinois, it was possible to administer the HSPQ to the entire seventh grade at one sitting in the school hall. In the other three samples it was given by classes. Parallel forms of the test (A and B) were administered to both American samples and to the British Secondary Modern sample. In the case of the other, more representative, British sample it was unfortunately only possible to administer Form A. Similarly, measures of school achievement were available for the two American samples and the Secondary Modern sample, but not for the second British sample.

The criteria of achievement available in the American schools were firstly the Stanford intermediate achievement test, Form K, which was taken by both schools, and which yields a total score, and six sub-scores, as follows: paragraph meaning, word meaning, spelling, language, arithmetic reasoning and arithmetic computation. Secondly, teacher ratings were obtained on the children's behaviour in school on a graphic seven-point scale.

The criteria of achievement available in the British Secondary Modern school sample were the results of the annual internal school examinations in English, Mathematics, History, Geography, Science and Art. The papers were set by the heads of departments in these subjects and all eight streams of children attempted the same papers. To aim at a standardisation of marking, one teacher was responsible for the marking of a particular question throughout all the streams. This procedure was not adopted specifically for this research, but was part of the annual promotion policy of the school involved.

Results

COMPARISON OF THE TWO AMERICAN GROUPS

Table 14.1 below shows for the two American schools the mean scores and standard deviation on the fourteen primary and the two second-order factors measured by the HSPQ.

TABLE 14.1

Mean Scores (HSPQ, Forms A and B)

	Factor	Springfield (N = 154)		Paxton (N = 123)		t	Significance of difference
		Mean	SD	Mean	SD		
Sociability	A	11·10	3·02	11·60	2·75	1·45	n.s.
Intelligence	B	14·11	2·48	13·68	2·39	1·46	n.s.
Ego-strength	C	8·92	2·96	10·47	2·49	4·74	0·0001
Excitability	D	9·60	2·98	9·35	2·62	0·73	n.s.
Assertion	E	8·89	2·77	9·27	2·89	1·05	n.s.
Enthusiasm	F	9·78	2·83	10·00	2·47	0·69	n.s.
Conscientiousness	G	12·56	3·18	12·15	2·91	1·12	n.s.
Adventurousness	H	8·39	2·92	9·56	2·56	3·56	0·001
Sensitivity	I	10·14	3·28	9·95	3·08	0·50	n.s.
Passive individualism	J	10·68	2·00	9·86	2·37	3·06	0·01
Timidity	O	10·68	3·02	9·42	2·75	3·64	0·001
Self-sufficiency	Q2	10·73	2·20	10·46	2·28	1·00	n.s.
Self-control	Q3	10·18	2·37	10·61	2·18	1·57	n.s.
Tenseness	Q4	9·32	2·73	8·68	2·61	1·99	0·05
Extraversion		69·81	10·78	73·86	10·64	3·12	0·01
Anxiety		109·47	18·74	101·74	15·60	3·76	0·001

The urban group (Springfield) is significantly more introverted and more anxious than the rural one. The mean difference in anxiety is particularly marked, not only in terms of the second-order factor, but also in the fact that of the five primary factors on which the groups differ, four (C−, H−, O, Q4) load anxiety, and in each case the difference indicates that the urban children score in the anxious direction.

A COMPARISON BETWEEN AMERICAN CHILDREN AND BRITISH SECONDARY MODERN CHILDREN

Table 14.2 shows a comparison between the total American sample and the British Secondary Modern school sample.

The marked difference in intelligence (B) is to be expected, since the American group covers the whole range of ability, whereas the British group is selected (or "non-selected"), and also rather younger. In addition the British children are seen to be markedly less sociable, more assertive, less conscientious, more timid and more tense, these last two factors (O and Q4) being the principal indicators of anxiety. In terms of the two second-order factors, they are considerably more introverted and more anxious.

TABLE 14.2

Mean Scores (HSPQ, Forms A and B)

	Factor	American Children (N = 277)		British Children (N = 230)		t	Significance of difference
		Mean	SD	Mean	SD		
Sociability	A	11·32	2·91	9·77	2·71	6·17	0·0001
Intelligence	B	13·92	2·44	11·92	2·60	8·85	0·0001
Ego-strength	C	9·58	2·89	9·07	2·60	2·10	0·05
Excitability	D	9·48	2·84	10·12	2·40	2·78	0·01
Assertion	E	9·08	2·83	11·13	2·57	8·51	0·0001
Enthusiasm	F	9·88	2·67	10·09	2·78	0·86	n.s.
Conscientiousness	G	12·34	3·10	10·63	2·76	6·55	0·0001
Adventurousness	H	8·90	2·84	8·53	2·49	1·56	n.s.
Sensitivity	I	10·06	3·19	10·41	2·92	1·29	n.s.
Passive individualism	J	10·32	2·21	10·11	2·35	1·02	n.s.
Timidity	O	10·09	2·99	11·24	2·69	4·58	0·0001
Self-sufficiency	Q2	10·59	2·27	10·64	2·35	0·24	n.s.
Self-control	Q3	10·38	2·30	9·68	2·58	3·20	0·01
Tenseness	Q4	9·04	2·69	10·24	2·46	5·26	0·0001
Extraversion		71·61	11·11	68·14	11·24	3·48	0·001
Anxiety		105·98	16·73	114·24	14·93	5·91	0·0001

Admittedly, the comparison is not entirely a straightforward one, since the British sample is entirely urban and does not contain children from secondary grammar or technical schools. But on the first point, it is plain that the British sample differs markedly not only from the total American sample, but from the American urban sample, and that in every case the differences are still in the same direction.

TABLE 14.3

Mean Scores (HSPQ, Form A only)

	Factor	American Children (N = 277)		British Children (N = 140)		t	Significance of difference
		Mean	SD	Mean	SD		
Sociability	A	5·22	1·74	4·74	1·81	2·61	0·01
Intelligence	B	7·12	1·65	6·92	1·91	1·05	n.s.
Ego-strength	C	4·91	1·80	4·87	1·57	0·23	n.s.
Excitability	D	5·08	1·65	5·04	1·72	0·23	n.s.
Assertion	E	4·76	1·86	5·66	1·62	5·11	0·0001
Enthusiasm	F	5·44	1·66	5·64	1·67	1·16	n.s.
Conscientiousness	G	6·13	1·74	5·19	1·44	5·84	0·0001
Adventurousness	H	4·69	1·83	4·61	1·94	0·41	n.s.
Sensitivity	I	4·52	1·98	4·01	1·89	2·55	0·05
Passive individualism	J	5·53	1·45	5·78	1·64	1·53	n.s.
Timidity	O	5·04	1·77	5·33	1·81	1·58	n.s.
Self-sufficiency	Q2	5·17	1·61	5·49	1·68	1·85	n.s.
Self-control	Q3	4·31	1·63	4·36	1·57	0·30	n.s.
Tenseness	Q4	4·61	1·70	4·59	1·61	0·12	n.s.
Extraversion		36·53	11·15	35·59	9·80	0·88	n.s.
Anxiety		55·24	7·40	55·71	7·88	0·59	n.s.

A COMPARISON BETWEEN AMERICAN CHILDREN AND A REPRESENTATIVE SAMPLE OF BRITISH SECONDARY SCHOOL CHILDREN (Table 14.3)

Perhaps the most striking feature of Table 14.3 is the confirmation of the very marked and highly significant difference already found between British and American children on factors E and G. The British children appear as very clearly more assertive and less conscientious. The lower sociability of British children is also confirmed, though less strikingly. The low score of the British children on factor I (sensitivity) is perhaps rather surprising. It is also interesting that (unlike the Secondary Modern group) to representative sample of British children does not differ significantly from the American children either in extraversion or anxiety.

THE RELATION BETWEEN PERSONALITY FACTORS AND SCHOOL ACHIEVEMENT

The product-moment correlation coefficients between the fourteen personality factors and the measures of school achievement are shown in Tables 14.4—14.6 following.

TABLE 14.4

The Relation of School Achievement to Fourteen Personality Factors Springfield, Illinois (N=153)

	Personality Factors													
	A	B	C	D	E	F	G	H	I	J	O	Q2	Q3	Q4
Total	17*	62†	02	–09	–22†	02	34†–01	08	06	–04	35†	18*–02
Paragraph meaning	15	57†	03	–08	–14	05	32†	08	–05	05	–09	35†	14	11
Word meaning	04	58†–02	–05	–08	–01	29†–05	–02	06	03	32†	13	–05
Spelling	25†	53†–03	–06	–30†	16*	33†–02	14	09	01	18*	05	06
Language	21†	53†	00	–12	–24†	02	34†–05	13	17*–02	22†	13	06
Arithmetic reasoning	19*	54†	04	–11	–10	–02	31†	00	–04	01	–03	35†	12	–05
Arithmetic computation	19*	46†–08	01	–22†	01	36†–04	00	03	–02	26†	03	–02
Teacher rating on behaviour record	13	18*–10	–16*–28†–09	18*	13	23†	03	–16*	15	26†	06

* Significant at 5 per cent level.
† Significant at 1 per cent level.

TABLE 14.5

The Relation of School Achievement to Fourteen Personality Factors Paxton, Illinois (N=124)

	Personality Factors													
	A	B	C	D	E	F	G	H	I	J	O	Q2	Q3	Q4
Total	12	51†	00	–01	–02	–08	18*	01	–20*	02	–11	15	10	–02
Paragraph meaning	19*	25†	03	–05	00	–09	17*–02	–14	–09	–11	19*	12	02
Word meaning	13	47†	13	–05	06	–09	21*	05	–21*–04	–17*	19*	09	–04
Spelling	09	45†–05	–07	–07	–15	23†	07	–01	–03	–04	10	09	–08
Language	11	43†–11	–03	–10	–04	14	–03	–12	–01	–09	–01	01	–02
Arithmetic reasoning	11	41†	03	–07	02	–01	10	13	–23†	06	–17*	11	10	–09
Arithmetic computation	15	32†	02	–07	00	–03	22*	08	–11	08	–21*	13	11	–12
Teacher rating on behaviour record	12	26†–04	–18*–14	04	16	–01	11	–12	–03	00	29†–01

* Significant at 5 per cent level.
† Significant at 1 per cent level.

TABLE 14.6

The Relation of School Achievement to Fourteen Personality Factors
Manchester (*N* = 230)

	Personality Factors													
	A	B	C	D	E	F	G	H	I	J	O	Q2	Q3	Q4
English	11	45†	–04	110	–01	–10	15*	–10	05	07	08	13*	–07	02
Maths	08	34†	03	–01	–07	–01	08	–01	03	00	03	15*	–04	–06
Science	–01	33†	14*	01	–05	–03	10	–05	–14*	02	–09	14*	01	–13*
History	–01	23†	09	09	–03	–03	02	–18†	–14*	–11	–01	14*	–06	–20
Geography	–10	26†	02	00	00	–08	10	–14*	–08	00	03	16*	07	–14*
Art	–07	08	16*	–16*	04	–11	22†	04	06	12	01	06	19†	–18†

* Significant at 5 per cent level.
† Significant at 1 per cent level.

The main features of these tables appear to be as follows:

(1) As in earlier researches, the correlations are not strikingly high. With the exception of factor B (intelligence), no factor yields a correlation of over 0·4. In general they are higher for the Springfield sample than for either the Paxton or the Manchester samples. This may very possibly be due to a greater standardisation of testing conditions, since the entire Springfield group was tested at one sitting in the school hall, whereas the other two groups were tested by classes.

(2) There is some consistent pattern as between the three samples. In particular, factors G and Q2 correlate consistently with all measures of achievement in all three groups. Of the twenty-two correlations involving factor G (conscientiousness), all are positive, and in the American groups the great majority are statistically significant. Twenty-one of the twenty-two correlations involving factor Q2 (self-sufficiency) are positive, and fourteen of these are significant. The role of these two factors is nearly equal. In the Springfield sample, both yield correlations of around 0·3, in the Paxton sample around 0·2, in the Manchester sample around 0·1.

(3) There is remarkably little differential prediction of the various aspects of achievement. In general, the factors such as G and Q2 which clearly predict success, predict it over the whole range of criteria. Similarly, the other factors, such as A (sociability) and E– (submissiveness) which predict to a lesser degree (also Q4 in the British sample), still do so, almost regardless of school subject. The teachers' ratings on behaviour record clearly stand in a different category in this respect, but even here intelligence, conscientiousness and self-sufficiency appear to play some part. But it is noticeable that Q3 (self-control) E– (submissiveness), and D– (lack of excitability) also correlate with behaviour rating in both samples. These correlations appear to make good psychological sense.

(4) Factor A (sociability) correlates positively (but low) with all criteria in both American samples, but yields no significant correlation in the British sample. It is possible and plausible that this represents a genuine cultural difference, though it is hard to be sure owing to

the general attenuation of correlations in the British group. This attenuation may be due either to the conditions of testing or to the lesser suitability of the questionnaire to British children.

Discussion

One obvious question comes to mind in connection with the results reported. To what extent were the national samples typical of children in the two countries?

Some further light can be thrown on this issue by a comparison of the results obtained for the American children with norms reported in the handbook of the test. Although there is naturally some deviation of our figures from these norms, inspection suggests that the national differences found may be real ones. If one were to substitute the handbook norms in Table 14.2 for the figures obtained from the combined American sample, every difference from the British Secondary Modern children (on the nine factors where significant differences were found) would still be in the same direction. To take one example, a striking difference was found on factor G (conscientiousness) between the American children ($M=12·34$) and the British Secondary Modern children ($M=10·63$). The corresponding mean score of the American group on whom the test was standardised was $12·2$.

Similar results hold for the comparison between the American children and the representative British sample on Form A only. If one substitutes the handbook norms on Form A for the mean scores obtained by the American children, the differences on the factors where significant differences were found would all be in the same direction. Strikingly enough, in the case of the two factors of assertion and conscientiousness, where very marked differences were found between the two groups, to substitute the handbook norms for the actual Illinois results would make these differences larger still. Admittedly the average difference in age between the American children and those in the second British sample (amounting to some eighteen months) impairs the comparison, but the results appear sufficiently clear-cut to indicate some genuine differences.

Although it has not been an aim of this paper directly to contrast Secondary Modern with Secondary Grammar children, it is interesting to compare our findings with those of Hallworth[11]. Hallworth points out that the British Psychological Society's report on Secondary School Selection states fairly categorically that there is considerably more worry and anxiety among Grammar than among Modern school pupils, and questions this statement in the light of his own findings, suggesting that the opposite may be true. Our own results, in which a Modern school group were significantly more anxious than American children, but in which no such difference was found for a representative sample, provide some indirect support for Hallworth's findings.

Turning to the correlations with measures of school achievement, one finds results that are promising and suggestive rather than conclusive. The coefficients of correlation are generally low, though frequently statistically significant. To a large extent this may be inherent in the method of the personality questionnaire which has long been an object of suspicion and of lively satirical attack by laymen (Whyte[12]). A particular deficiency of the HSPQ may be the obverse of its merit, the fact that by aiming to measure a large number of factors in a comparatively short testing time, it necessarily sacrifices some precision on each factor. Thus factor B (intelligence) yields lower correlations than would be expected from a full-scale intelligence test. The HSPQ was not constructed with the sole aim of predicting school achievement, but with the much wider one of providing a general picture of the respondent's personality pattern. It might well be a useful task for future research to concentrate on those factors (such as G and Q2) which appear to be most directly related to attainment, and to develop fuller and longer scales for the specific purpose of predicting attainment.

Conclusions

(1) In Illinois, U.S.A., urban children were found to be more introverted and markedly more anxious than rural children.

(2) Children at a Secondary Modern school in Lancashire were more introverted and very clearly more anxious than the Illinois children.

(3) When a second British sample, which covered the whole ability range, was compared with the Illinois group, no significant differences were found on the factors of extraversion or anxiety.

(4) The American children were found to be very significantly more sociable, less assertive and more conscientious than either British group.

(5) Apart from intelligence, two of the remaining thirteen factors measured by the HSPQ correlate fairly consistently with school attainment. These are G (conscientiousness) and Q2 (self-sufficiency). Among the American children, factor A (sociability) was the next most consistent predictor.

References

[1] G. MIDDLETON and G. M. GUTHRIE, "Personality Syndromes and Academic Achievement", *Journal of Educational Psychology*, 1959, **60**, pp. 66-69.

[2] R. B. CATTELL, H. BELOFF, and R. W. COAN, *Handbook for the I.P.A.T. High School Personality Questionnaire*, Institute for Personality and Ability Testing, Champaign, 1958.

[3] I. SARNOFF, F. LIGHTHALL, R. WAITE, K. DAVIDSON and S. A. SARASON, "A Cross-Cultural Study of Anxiety Among American and English Children", *Journal of Educational Psychology*, 1958, **49**, pp. 129-36.

[4] R. B. CATTELL and F. W. WARBURTON, "A Cross-Cultural Comparison of Patterns of Extraversion and Anxiety", *British Journal of Psychology*, 1961, **52**, pp. 3-16.

[5] W. FURNEAUX, *The Selection of University Students*, Report to the Imperial College of Science, London, 1957.

[6] F. N. COX, "Correlates of General and Test Anxiety in Children", *Australian Journal of Psychology*, 1960, **12**, pp. 169-77.

[7] R. R. GROOMS and N. S. ENDLER, "The Effect of Anxiety on Academic Achievement", *Journal of Educational Psychology*, 1960, **51**, pp. 229-304.

[8] R. LYNN, "Temperamental Characteristics Related to Disparity of Attainment in Reading and Arithmetic", *British Journal of Educational Psychology*, 1957, **27**, pp. 62-68.

[9] A. W. ANDERSON, "Personality Traits of Western Australian University Entrants", *Australian Journal of Psychology*, 1960, **12**, pp. 4-9.

[10] F. W. WARBURTON, "The Measurement of Personality—III", *Educational Research*, 1962, **4**, pp. 193-206.

[11] H. J. HALLWORTH, "Anxiety in Secondary School Children", *British Journal of Educational Psychology*, 1961, **31**, pp. 281-91.

[12] W. H. WHYTE, *The Organization Man*, Simon & Schuster, New York, 1956.

ACKNOWLEDGEMENT

The American results were obtained as part of a research supported through the Co-operative Research Programme of the Office of Education, U.S. Department of Health, Education and Welfare (Project number 701 (8383)), and under the direction of Professor R. B. Cattell of the University of Illinois. The writers' thanks are also due to the Headmasters of the schools in Paxton and Springfield, Illinois, and of those in Manchester for their helpful cooperation.

Chapter 15

The Relationship Between Personality Characteristics and Scholastic Success in Eleven-Year-Old Children

JAMES RUSHTON
Department of Education, The University, Manchester

Teacher ratings of personality and ability on 458 children aged 11 years were obtained as were their scores on a personality questionnaire and tests of cognitive ability. The scores were intercorrelated. The major finding was that, according to the CPQ test and teacher ratings, well adjusted, extravert children have higher scholastic attainment.

Introduction

For a number of years the idea that personality factors play an important part in scholastic success has been accepted. There remains the problem of identifying and measuring the factors which lead to success or failure. Standardised questionnaires provide a useful instrument for assessing large samples and the Children's Personality Questionnaire (Cattell and Porter[1]) appears to be one of the more promising instruments available for use with children because:

(*a*) It provides measures on fourteen primary factors (the second-order factors—anxiety and extraversion—are derived from weighted sums of the first-order factors).

(*b*) The factors have been derived from a considerable body of research and they correspond broadly to those found in adults.

The majority of studies published to date are concerned with the two broad personality traits of anxiety-adjustment and extraversion-introversion. Nearly all are based on samples of adults or older children; a

From the *British Journal of Educational Psychology*, 1966, **36**, pp. 178-84. Reprinted by permission of James Rushton and the *British Journal of Educational Psychology*.

good proportion are American and much of the evidence is conflicting. The evidence arraigns itself in this way. Of the twenty-seven researches so far reported which study the relationship between anxiety (neuroticism) and academic achievement, eleven researchers favour the hypothesis that anxiety (neuroticism) is positively connected with academic achievement and sixteen suggest the contrary. Considering only studies based on the questionnaires of Cattell, Eysenck and Guilford, we find six out of fifteen linking neuroticism with achievement. The over-riding impression is that wheneven the training course is particularly severe, neuroticism tends to be a positive influence. In other words, "tensed up" people are more able to deal with a tense situation.

However, if the evidence is kept strictly to work done with children, eleven out of thirteen studies connect stability, as opposed to anxiety, with ability, or seven out of eight if work not based on standardised questionnaire measures is excluded. Thus, in twenty-eight instances out of forty-two (or some 70 per cent of the researches studied) stability or adjustment is positively connected with academic achievement.

Turning to the relationship between introversion-extraversion and scholastic performance, we find seventeen out of nineteen showing a significant connection between introversion and scholastic success. It must be stressed, however, that most of these researches are with older children or adults. Both Warburton[2] and Butcher[3] are of the opinion that research indicates that in junior school children extraversion may be a positive influence in scholastic success. Banks[4] supports this theory.

The experiment was designed with the following aims in view:

(*a*) To investigate the relationship between personality assessments as measured on an objective questionnaire and cognitive ability measures as used in an actual 11-plus examination.

(*b*) To study the relationship between teacher ratings of personality and ability and the objective personality questionnaire.

Method

A sample of 458 boys and girls, aged 10-11 years, was drawn from fourteen county primary schools approximately representing the different socio-economic strata and school size in a large county borough. They also had, without exception, verbal reasoning quotients of 105 and above.

(*a*) The children were tested on each of the following tests:

    (i) Children's Personality Questionnaire (Cattell) Forms A and B.

    (ii) Moray House Verbal Reasoning Test No. 63.

    (iii) Moray House Arithmetic Test No. 30.

    (iv) Moray House English Test No. 30.

    (v) Moray House Spatial Test No. 2.

    (vi) A Teachers' Rating Scale of Fourteen Personality and Ability Traits.

(*b*) Treatment of Data.

The data used in the experiments were of four types:

(i) Personality scores from the children's Personality Questionnaire. These data consisted of thirteen first-order factors
(factor B intelligence was withdrawn because the Moray
House Verbal Reasoning Quotient is an adequate measure
of this ability) and two second-order factors.

(ii) Ability measures on the Moray House battery.

(iii) Teacher ratings on a Fourteen-Point Scale. For each of the
fourteen traits a raw score total was converted to a standard
score incorporating a correction for differences between age
groups.

(iv) Pass-Fail.

All of the above scores were converted to normalised T scores
because many of the teacher ratings were heavily skewed in a negative
direction. Means, standard deviations and intercorrelations were then
calculated. All calculations with the exception of conversion to T scores
were carried out on the Atlas Electronic Computer of the University of
Manchester.

Results

THE RELATIONSHIP BETWEEN COGNITIVE ABILITY MEASURES AND THE PERSONALITY VARIABLES FROM CATTELL'S CPQ

Table 15.1 below shows the product moment coefficients of correlation
between the cognitive ability measures, the pass-fail dichotomy and
Cattell's personality measures.

TABLE 15.1

Correlations Between Cattell's Personality Variables, Cognitive Abilities and Pass-Fail Dichotomy

		Verbal Reasoning	Arithmetic	English	Spatial	School Record	Pass vs. Fail
A+	Sociability						
C+	Ego Strength	145	144	149	124*	202	−219
D+	Excitability						
E+	Dominance			145		096*	
F+	Surgency	148	121*	160		112	−142
G+	Conscientiousness	180	164	135*		183	−132*
D+	Adventurousness		115*				
I+	Sensitivity				134*		
J+	Passive Individualism						
N+	Shrewdness						
O+	Guilt Proneness						
Q3+	Self-Control					119*	
Q4+	Tenseness			−102*			
A—A	Anxiety	−200	−149	−162	−103*	−195	147
E—I	Extraversion	161	110*	130*		145	−138
Nr	Neuroticism	−143	−153	−141		−157	167

* Denotes significance at the 5 per cent level.
N = 458. (All correlations shown are significant at the 5 per cent or 1 per cent level.)

The following points ensue:

(i) The second-order factor of anxiety clearly has a negative correlation with verbal reasoning, arithmetic, English and school record and failure on the pass-fail dichotomy. This implies that the less anxious better adjusted child is most likely to succeed in school work at this age.

(ii) Extraversion, the other major second-order factor, correlates positively with verbal reasoning quotient, school record, arithmetic and English and success (on the pass-fail dichotomy). Thus, at this age, extraversion favours scholastic success.

(iii) The "experimental" second-order factor of Neuroticism follows the pattern of anxiety fairly closely. It is clear that low neuroticism makes for success in school just as does low anxiety.

(iv) The primary factors of Ego Strength, Surgency and Conscientiousness appear to assist all work in the cognitive field.

In summary, the stable extravert child is the one who, on these results, succeeds at his school work.

THE RELATIONSHIP BETWEEN CATTELL'S PERSONALITY VARIABLES AND TEACHER RATINGS OF PERSONALITY AND ABILITY (Table 15.2)

The outstanding features of this table are:

(i) On the second-order factor of anxiety, children with low scores are rated by teachers as more fitted for an academic secondary education than others.

(ii) Extraversion correlates positively with teacher ratings of ambition, relations with seniors and perseverance. On these three important aspects the more extraverted children are rated by their teachers as being well fitted for an academic secondary education.

(iii) The second-order factor of neuroticism confirms the finding that the more anxious children are less able academically.

(iv) The first-order factors are confirmed to some extent by the teacher ratings. In particular, Ego Strength (C+) as measured by the questionnaire is a trait which teachers pick out, under different names of the fourteen traits, as an important factor in scholastic success. In a similar way, conscientiousness (G+) self control (Q3+) and sensitivity (I+) were also selected as traits which have a great influence on school success.

(v) It is also striking that children who rate themselves as surgent and enthusiastic, are rated by their teachers as ambitious and quick at their school tasks. Adventurousness also correlates positively with speed of working and perseverance. Tenseness has a negative connection with leadership, as is *prima facie* plausible. As in earlier researches, the coefficients of correlation in both of these tables are low as compared with correlations between ability measures.

TABLE 15.2
Correlations Between Cattell's Personality Factors and Teacher Ratings of Scholastic and Personality Traits: Total and Sex

	1 Ambition	2 Alertness	3 Accuracy	4 Industriousness	5 Method	6 Speed of Working	7 Leadership	8 Relationship with Seniors	9 Relationship with Contemporaries	10 Cooperativeness	11 Self-consciousness	12 Perseverance	13 Reliability	14 Emotional Stability	15 Special Abilities, Arts, Crafts, etc.
A+ Sociability	096*							098*	121*		097*	166	162		
C+ Ego Strength	174	165	181	132*	135*	121*	114*	245	121*	144	167		-130*		193
D+ Excitability		-124*			-116*				-120*						
E+ Dominance															
F+ Surgency	136					189	205	165							
G+ Conscientiousness	190	200	191	208	178	103*	209		103*		098*	170	098*		
H+ Adventurousness	095*	104*	140	107*		162	115*					153			
I+ Sensitivity		094*		191	135*		136		102*		177		128*		
J+ Passive Individualism		-091*	-100*									103*	-120*		
N+ Shrewdness			-101*												
O+ Guilt Proneness			-096*				-100*								
Q3+ Self-Control			136	112*					114*		117*		118*		
Q4+ Tenseness							-100*		-129*						136
A-A Anxiety	-172	-195	-190	-193		-114*		-159	-131*		-146	-106*	-181		
E-I Extraversion	142	107*	114			135*	-123*	138			113*	169			
Nr Neuroticism	-151	-162						-137					-093*		

* Denotes correlation is significant at the 5 per cent level.
(Note the decimal points have been left out of this table.)
N = 458. (All the correlations are significant at the 5 per cent or 1 per cent level.)

Discussion

To a teacher or educational psychologist, it seems obvious that at given levels of intelligence the well-adjusted child should have a superior academic record to the anxious child. One of the findings of this research is quite definitely that in children of 11 years of age stability is positively correlated with academic success. This finding conflicts with those of Furneaux[5] and Lynn[6], but they were working with university students. It agrees, however with the findings of Hallworth[7], Butcher, Ainsworth and Nesbitt[8], Lunzer[9] and Callard and Goodfellow.[10] Explanations of the positive association between stability and academic achievement could be that well-adjusted children are not distracted to the same degree by their personal problems. Also that younger children are not affected to the same extent by personal sensitivity and ambition which could lead to anxiety, drive and success in older pupils and students.

Another finding was that extraverted children were more able scholastically than others. This finding is in direct conflict with most other researches in this field. Furneaux[5], Lynn[6], Cattell[11] and Holmes[12] all found that introversion was of positive help in academic pursuits. Banks[4] supports the writer's view. It is feasible that the thoughtful consideration of problems is too fragmentary to be of any value scholastically or that extraverted children make contacts more easily and become socially and mentally mature earlier, thus adapting themselves to the requirements of the classroom. With older children, however, one would expect the hard thinking, well read introvert to come into his own.

It would be interesting to see if the scholastically superior children who are extraverted at the age of 11 are still classed as extravert at say the age of 15 or whether bright extraverts at age 11 tend to become bright introverts at later ages.

It is noteworthy that teachers indirectly relate extraversion and stability to school attainment as their ratings correlate positively with the questionnaire factors. Thus, the academically successful child both rates himself and is rated by his teachers as extraverted and stable, although neither the child nor the teacher is consciously aware of the importance of these two major factors.

Conclusions

(1) According to the CPQ test the well-adjusted, extraverted children tend to have higher scholastic attainment as assessed by Moray House attainment tests.

(2) With regard to the correlations between the teacher ratings of personality, the main results confirm the first finding since it is the stable extravert children who have superior attainment.

In respect of stability the major findings in terms of primary factors are:

(i) That emotional maturity (C+) at this age would appear to assist children in scholastic pursuits.

(ii) That the more relaxed (Q4 —) children tend to be better at English.

(iii) That perseverance (G+) is positively related to success in school work at this age.

In respect of extraversion the major findings are :

(i) That teachers tend to rate children who are more "easy going" (A+) as more suitable for an academic career than others.

(ii) That the more dominant (E+) children tend to be more proficient at arithmetic.

(iii) That "happy-go-lucky" (F+) children appear to be selected as more likely to benefit from an academic secondary education.

(3) The main relationship between the personality questionnaire results and the ratings of personality made by teachers show:

(i) That internally restrained (G+) children are rated by teachers as more persistent.

(ii) That children with better self-control (Q3 +) have better school records.

References

[1] R. B. CATTELL and R. B. PORTER, *Handbook for the I.P.A.T. Children's Personality Questionnaire*, Institute for Personality and Ability Testing, Champaign, 1959.

[2] F. W. WARBURTON, H. J. BUTCHER and G. M. FORREST, "Predicting Student Performance in a University Department of Education", *British Journal of Educational Psychology*, 1963, 33, pp. 68-80.

[3] H. J. BUTCHER, "A Study of Attainment, Personality and Motivation in School Children." Unpublished report, 1963.

[4] J. BANKS, "The Relationship between Problem Solving in Arithmetic and Correct Attainment, Intelligence and Personality Characteristics in Junior School Children". M.Ed. Thesis, University of Manchester, 1964.

[5] W. D. FURNEAUX, "Student Selection," Report to the Imperial College of Science and Technology, quoted in Lynn[6].

[6] R. LYNN, "Two Personality Characteristics Related to Academic Achievement", *British Journal of Educational Psychology*, 1959, 29, pp. 213-17.

[7] H. J. HALLWORTH, "Anxiety in Secondary School Children", *British Journal of Educational Psychology*, 1961, 31, pp. 281-91.

[8] H. J. BUTCHER, M. E. AINSWORTH and J. E. NESBITT, "Personality Factors and School Achievement—a Comparison of British and American Children", *British Journal of Educational Psychology*, 1963, 33, pp. 276-86.

[9] E. A. LUNZER, "Aggressive and Withdrawing Children in the Normal School", *British Journal of Educational Pyschology*, 1960, 30, pp. 119-23.

[10] M. P. CALLARD and C. L. GOODFELLOW, "Three Experiments Using the Junior Maudsley Personality Inventory. Neuroticism and Extraversion in School Boys as measured by J.M.P.I.", *British Journal of Educational Psychology*, 1962, 32, pp. 241-51.

[11] R. B. CATTELL, "Predicting Success in Academic Aspects of Military Training Schools", *I.P.A.T. Information Bulletin*, No. 4, 1960, Institute for Personality and Ability Testing, Champaign. Department of Psychology, University of Illinois.

[12] F. J. HOLMES, "Predicting Academic Success on a General College Curriculum", *I.P.A.T. Information Bulletin*, No. 4, 1960, Institute for Personality and Ability Testing, Champaign.

Chapter 16

Two Personality Characteristics Related to Academic Achievement

R. LYNN
Exeter University

Experimental studies suggest that capacity for sustained work depends largely on an individual's level of drive and rate of accumulation of inhibition. This work implies that good academic achievers should be characterised by high drive levels and a slow rate of accumulating inhibition. The Maudsley Personality Inventory measures these two personality dimensions and a comparison of the scores of university students with those of controls confirms both predictions.

Introduction

The theories of behaviour built up by experimentalists (e.g., Hull[1]) have now reached a stage where there is broad agreement on certain general principles. At this point the findings of laboratory experimentation should be of considerable use to the various fields of applied psychology, and, in fact, considerable use of behaviour theory as an explanatory device has been made in the areas of personality development (e.g. Dollard and Miller;[2] Sears, Maccoby and Levin[3]), psychotherapy (Davis,[4] Eysenck[5]), and individual differences (Eysenck[5]). As yet, however, and with one notable exception (Peel[6]), rather little use of behaviour theory has been made in educational psychology. The present paper is concerned with two predictions from behaviour theory to the problem of individual personality differences in capacity for academic work.

It is clear that people differ considerably in their capacity for sustained and concentrated work and it seems likely that this personality characteristic contributes to good educational attainment, perhaps to a considerable degree. In behaviour theory terms, sustained work is

From the *British Journal of Educational Psychology*, 1959, **29**, pp. 213-16. Reprinted by permission of R. Lynn and the *British Journal of Educational Psychology*.

largely dependent on two factors, namely, the strength of drive and the accumulation of inhibition as work proceeds. Individuals with a capacity for sustained work should, therefore, be characterised in the following way: (1) they should have high drives; (2) they should accumulate reactive inhibition slowly with continuous work. Some of the recent studies of Eysenck[5] simplify the testing of these predictions. In this work, Eysenck has identified his personality dimension of neuroticism with autonomic drive, and that of extraversion with the fast accumulation and slow dissipation of reactive inhibition. There is now a considerable amount of experimental evidence supporting this theory, for which the reader is referred to the original reports (e.g., Eysenck[5]). If Eysenck's theory is accepted, the predictions about educational attainment can be stated as follows: good educational attainers should (1) score high on neuroticism; (2) low on extraversion.

Several recent studies have produced evidence supporting this theory. The most extensive of these is that of Furneaux,[7] who has shown that students who do well at university score more highly on neuroticism and lower on extraversion. He also puts forward the interesting view that extraversion only begins to have a detrimental effect on educational attainment at the university level. His argument on this aspect of the question is as follows: if candidates who are accepted and rejected for university places are considered, their extraversion scores are very similar. However, since their educational attainment differs (this being largely the basis of acceptance or rejection), it appears that at the level of university entrance extraversion is not related to educational attainment. Furneaux suggests that the explanation for this lies in the stricter supervision of school life in which the tendency of the extravert to dissipate his energies is held in check.

A corroboratory study of the introversion-extraversion finding has been reported by Broadbent[8]. Students graduating at Cambridge were divided into those obtaining good and poor degrees, and their level of extraversion assessed by means of the triple tester; this test showed that students who do well were significantly more introverted than those who do badly. This study also showed that the two groups of students did not differ in intelligence as assessed by the A.H.4 test and suggests, therefore, that introversion-extraversion acts independently of intelligence in affecting educational attainment.

Several studies have been made of the relation of educational attainment to anxiety, with rather conflicting results. The concept of anxiety is rather an unsatisfactory one, since although it is largely a measure of neuroticism (autonomic drive), it is also related to introversion. Hence, the theory would predict that high anxious subjects should do well in tasks where sustained work is required, although it is not certain how far this is due to neuroticism or introversion. Some evidence in support of this prediction has been presented elsewhere (Lynn[9]).

The present paper reports findings extending the work of Furneaux and Broadbent. Essentially, these investigators have shown that good students differ from poor students in the expected directions of introversion and neuroticism. The theory should also predict that students as a whole should differ from other young people on these two dimensions.

The Investigation

Levels of neuroticism and extraversion were assessed in university students and controls by means of the Maudsley Personality Inventory (see Eysenck[10]). University students were all in their first year at university; mean age of women = 18·8, mean age of men = 19·2. Controls used were (a) sixty-seven female occupational therapy students

TABLE 16.1

	Norms	Apprentices	University Students
Men:			
Number	200	100	115
Neuroticism	17·8	21·2	25·5
Extraversion	24·6	29·3	22·4
	Norms	O.Ts.	Students
Women:			
Number	200	67	96
Neuroticism	19·4	23·8	28·2
Extraversion	25·2	28·5	22·9

of the same age (mean age = 18·5) and social background as the female university students but differing in academic motivation; (b) 100 male apprentices aged 16-19 years whose scores on neuroticism and extraversion were taken from a study by Field[11]. There may have been some group difference in intelligence, but since there is virtually no correlation between the two personality dimensions and intelligence, this difference is probably of little significance. However, the possibility of intelligence affecting extraversion and neuroticism scores deserves further scrutiny. The norms of the questionnaire are also used as a control, although these are probably less satisfactory because there may be some tendency for different age groups to score differently.

The results are presented in Table 16.1. All the differences are in the predicted directions and are significant at the 0·05 level, as tested by the calculation of the standard errors of the differences between the means.

Discussion

The results support the two predictions at a significant level and extend the findings of Furneaux and Broadbent. Moreover, they show that extraversion has wider detrimental effects on educational attainment than Furneaux concludes on the basis of his work and that these effects manifest themselves below the level of university extrance. This conclusion follows from the quite large differences in extraversion between the university students and the occupational therapists and apprentices. Since university entrance is obtained largely on performance in "A" level, the results suggest that educational attainment at school is substantially affected by the introversion-extraversion dimension. Furneaux's findings of the small difference between accepted and rejected candidates is probably due to the fact that the rejected candidates must have been quite good attainers to be candidates for university entrance at all; further, the small difference he did obtain was in the expected direction, i.e., rejected candidates were more extraverted.

The finding that university students score significantly more highly on neuroticism than normal groups is perhaps surprising in view of Terman's[12] widely accepted finding that highly talented young Americans are better adjusted than the normal population. There are now a large number of studies on this subject and the results are conflicting, so that it is becoming increasingly evident that the findings obtained depend on the measuring instrument used for assessing "neuroticism" or "maladjustment". The present finding adds weight to the studies already existing which suggest that Terman's findings cannot be generalised too widely.

The findings suggest a further prediction concerning sex differences in personality and attainment. The present results confirm the common finding that women score more highly on tests of neuroticism and anxiety (e.g., Terman and Tyler[13]). Hence, it seems likely that if intelligence and extraversion are held constant, women should, by virtue of their higher level of neuroticism, be better academic attainers than men. As far as university students are concerned, this is perhaps not an easy prediction to test. For example, the fact that at Oxford women obtain a higher proportion of first class degrees than men is doubtless due in part to greater selectivity of intake. However, a large number of studies have shown that at the age of eleven, girls are significantly better attainers than boys (e.g., Yates and Pidgeon[14]). This could be explained in terms of their higher drive level.

It may be thought that the positive association of academic attainment with neuroticism presents a curious contrast with the results of laboratory experiments, in which it is generally found that high drive levels impair the learning of complex tasks. It seems that neuroticism has two different effects on attainment, a disorganising one on learning and performance in stress situations but a facilitating one in so far as it motivates sustained work. Further, at the educational levels of the university and school sixth form, its disorganising effects seem to be more than compensated for by its motivating powers. How far this is true at earlier educational levels seems to be a question well worth investigation.

References

[1] C. HULL, *A Behavior System*, Yale University Press, New Haven, 1952.

[2] J. DOLLARD and N. E. MILLER, *Personality and Psychotherapy*, McGraw-Hill, New York, 1950.

[3] R. R. SEARS, E. E. MACCOBY and H. LEVIN, *Patterns of Child Rearing*, Row Peterson and Co., New York, 1957.

[4] D. RUSSELL DAVIS, *Introduction to Psychopathology*, Oxford University Press, London, 1957.

[5] H. J. EYSENCK, *The Dynamics of Anxiety and Hysteria*, Routledge and Kegan Paul, London, 1957.

[6] E. A. PEEL, *The Psychological Basis of Education*, Oliver & Boyd, Edinburgh, 1956.

[7] W. D. FURNEAUX, Report to Imperial College of Science and Technology, 1957.

[8] D. E. BROADBENT, *Perception and Communication*, Pergamon Press, London, 1958.

[9] R. LYNN, "Personality Factors in Reading Achievement", *Proceedings of the Royal Society of Medicine*, 1955, **48**, 996-98.

[10] H. J. EYSENCK, "The Questionnaire Measurement of Neuroticism and Extraversion", *Rivista di Psicologica*, 1956, **50**, pp. 113-40.

[11] J. G. FIELD, "The Personalities of Criminals". Paper read to the Annual Conference of British Psychological Society, 1959.

[12] L. M. TERMAN, *Genetic Studies of Genius*, Stanford University Press, Stanford, 1925.

[13] L. M. TERMAN and L. E. TYLER, "Psychological Sex Differences", in L. Carmichael (Ed.), *Manual of Child Psychology*, John Wiley & Sons, New York, 1954.

[14] A. YATES and D. A. PIDGEON, *Admission to Grammar Schools*, Newnes, London, 1957.

Chapter 17

Personality Factors and Academic Performance

R. D. SAVAGE
University of New England

Experimental studies have suggested that personality factors, in particular neuroticism and extraversion, are important determinants of academic performance. The Maudsley Personality Inventory was given to first-year university students over three years and scores on this were related to academic performance at the end of their first year. The results showed that this 'Australian university population had higher mean neuroticism and extraversion scores than the norms for the test. Analysis of variance and correlation techniques showed that high scores on both factors were negatively related to academic performance.

Introduction

There has been much speculation concerning the relationship between personality and academic success. Two personality factors frequently postulated as contributing to academic achievement are neuroticism and extraversion. These may be measured by the Maudsley Personality Inventory. Eysenckian theory predicts that good educational attainers should (1) score high on neuroticism and (2) score low on extraversion. In addition, it may be that, though successful students may have high neuroticism scores compared with the general population norms, excessively high neuroticism may be detrimental to academic success.

Several recent studies, particularly those by Furneaux[1] at London University, Broadbent[2] at Cambridge, and Lynn[3] at Exeter have confirmed the Eysenckian predictions that high drive level in terms of low extraversion are beneficial to academic success.

The present investigation was conducted on first year Arts students at University of New England, Australia, between 1959-1961. It was hypothesised that (1) the higher the success of the student the lower the extraversion score; (2) the mean neuroticism score of the group will

From the *British Journal of Educational Psychology*, 1962, **32**, pp. 251-53. Reprinted by permission of R. D. Savage and the *British Journal of Educational Psychology*.

be higher than that for a general population; (3) the higher the academic success of the students, the lower the neuroticism score. The third prediction stems from a development of Eysenck's basic postulate to allow for a U-shaped relationship between neuroticism and performance. An optimum level of performance may be related to an optimum drive level for a task of given difficulty.

Method

One-hundred and sixty-eight students, male and female, entering the Arts Faculty of University of New England in 1959, 1960, 1961, were given the Maudsley Personality Inventory (Eysenck[4]) in their second term. The neuroticism and extraversion scores of each student were related to the results obtained in the annual examinations. All students in this study attempted four first-year subjects within the Arts Faculty curriculum. The students were divided into five groups according to the number of passes out of four obtained in the final examinations: group 1—no passes, group 2—one pass and so on. Finally, analyses of variance were performed on the neuroticism and extraversion scores of the five groups. In addition, mean neuroticism and extraversion scores were correlated with academic success.

Results

The mean neuroticism score for this university population was $27 \cdot 7$. The neuroticism scores of groups 1, 2, 3, 4 and 5 were subjected to analysis of variance. The means for the groups were 40, $31 \cdot 2$, $27 \cdot 1$, $28 \cdot 1$ and $26 \cdot 2$ respectively. The variances between groups were significant at the 1 per cent level (Table 17.1). There was a negative correlation of $-0 \cdot 9$ which is significant at the 5 per cent level, between the mean neuroticism score for each group and academic success.

TABLE 17.1
Analysis of Variance of Neuroticism Scores

	Sum of squares	Degrees of freedom	Mean square	F ratio
Total variance	16843	167	—	—
Variance between groups	1416	4	354·0	3·74
Variance within groups	15427	163	94·6	—

The mean extraversion score for the population was $27 \cdot 3$. Analysis of variance of the extraversion scores showed mean scores of $36 \cdot 17$, $35 \cdot 14$, $28 \cdot 18$, $25 \cdot 5$ and $26 \cdot 1$ for groups 1, 2, 3, 4 and 5 respectively. The variances between groups were significant at the 1 per cent level (Table 17.2). The correlation between the mean extraversion score for each group and academic success ($-0 \cdot 9$) was significant at the 5 per cent level.

TABLE 17.2
Analysis of Variance of Extraversion Scores

	Sum of squares	Degrees of freedom	Mean square	F ratio
Total variance	13518	167	—	—
Variance between groups	1608	4	402·0	4·9
Variance within groups	12110	163	84·3	—

Discussion

The results of this investigation show that neuroticism and extraversion scores on the Maudsley Personality Inventory are significantly related to academic performance. The mean neuroticism and extraversion scores for this university population were significantly higher than the English or American norms for the MPI (Eysenck[4]) and comparable to those found by Lynn[3] for English university students.

The positive association between neuroticism and academic failure does not follow the results of Furneaux[1], Lynn[3] and others. Groups 3 and 4, who passed three and four subjects out of four had a mean neuroticism score significantly above the norm for the test. Groups 1, 2 and 3, however, had significantly higher neuroticism scores than the other two groups. These higher scores tended to impair performance. It may be suggested that an optimum level of neuroticism exists for successful academic achievement and that there is a U-shaped relationship between the variables.

The relationship found between extraversion and academic performance confirmed the results of Furneaux[1], Broadbent[2] and Lynn[3], with British university subjects. The most successful group was that with the lowest extraversion scores and the other groups ordered in the predicted direction.

The interesting problem still exists as to the interaction of neuroticism and extraversion in relation to academic performance. Further investigation of this is necessary. The present results suggest that academic performance X may be related to a neuroticism score A plus an extraversion score B, or a neuroticism score B plus an extraversion score A.

References

[1] W. D. FURNEAUX, Report to Imperial College of Science and Technology, 1957.
[2] D. E. BROADBENT, *Perception and Communication*, Pergamon Press, London, 1958.
[3] R. LYNN, "Two Personality Characteristics Related to Academic Performance", *British Journal of Educational Psychology*, 1959, **31**, pp. 213-16.
[4] H. J. EYSENCK, *The Dynamics of Anxiety and Hysteria*, Routledge and Kegan Paul, London, 1957.

Chapter 18

Neuroticism and School Attainment—a Linear Relationship?

N. J. ENTWISTLE* and SHIRLEY CUNNINGHAM
Department of Education, Aberdeen University

In a follow-up study 2,995 Aberdeen children aged about 13 years were given the Junior Eysenck Personality Inventory. School attainment was measured by teachers' average rank order in class, scaled on a verbal reasoning test. The relationships between attainment and the personality dimensions of neuroticism and extraversion were examined. Evidence is presented which suggests that the relationship between neuroticism and attainment is linear; high attainment in this age-group was associated with stability. The results for extraversion showed a sex difference, which may explain earlier conflicting findings. Girls who were stable extraverts and boys who were stable introverts formed superior groups. These relationships were also present among the brightest children.

Introduction

The relationships between academic attainment and scores on the personality inventories devised by Eysenck and Cattell have been investigated for both students and school children. The findings for these two populations show distinct differences.

At university level, Furneaux[1] reported that a group of "neurotic introverts" had the lowest failure rate in examinations. "Stable extroverts" had the highest failure rate. Kelvin and his co-workers[2] confirmed the superiority of the "neurotic introverts" but found that a group of student failures tended to be "neurotic extraverts". Also at university level, Lynn and Gordon[3] suggested that the Yerkes-Dodson "law" might indicate a non-linear relationship between anxiety or neuroticism and intelligence test scores, both high and low anxiety being associated

From the *British Journal of Educational Psychology*, 1968, **38**, pp. 123-32. Reprinted by permission of N. J. Entwistle, Shirley Cunningham and the *British Journal of Educational Psychology*.
* Now at Department of Educational Research, University of Lancaster.

with below average scores. They showed a regression curve of matrices score on neuroticism, which was of the expected inverted-U shape. But this curve was derived from a total group of only sixty students.

Among school children different results have been obtained. Rushton,[4] using Cattell's Children's Personality Questionnaire, found that the second-order factors of both anxiety and neuroticism correlated negatively with verbal reasoning score and school record, whereas extraversion showed a positive correlation with school attainment. Again, Hallworth[5] showed that teachers apparently base their personality ratings on the two main dimensions of social extraversion and emotional stability. Both these dimensions showed a positive correlation with school attainment. A conflicting finding was reported by Child[6] using the Junior Maudsley scale. He found that stable intraversion was related to high achievement in a sample which was not strictly representative.

Correlational studies assume linear relationships between the variables being investigated. Eysenck and White[7] suggested that the low values of the correlation coefficients between personality and intellectual measures in many studies might be caused by a non-linearity of relationship, similar to that found by Lynn and Gordon[3]. In the same article, Eysenck and White presented evidence which led them to suggest that children of different personality types may also have different intellectual structures. It might thus be possible to find different relationships between intelligence and personality, when different types of test were used. There might also be different relationships between these variables at different intellectual levels, which, in turn, might explain the differences between results obtained with university students and with school children.

The present study is based on data collected as part of an investigation into the age of transfer to secondary education in Scotland. The initial stages of this longitudinal study have already been reported (Nisbet and Entwistle[8]). The availability of JEPI scores and intellectual test scores on a nearly complete age-group of 13-year-olds suggested this digression from the main purpose of the follow-up study.

The previous results from studies of schol children raised the following questions. These also formed the hypotheses to be tested. (1) Is school attainment negatively related to neuroticism and positively related to extraversion, as measured by the JEPI? But (2) are the true relationships both non-linear? (3) Is there any sex difference in these relationships? (4) At the higher levels of attainment, do the "neurotic introverts" form a superior group compared with other personality types?

Method

The original age-group tested in 1964 consisted of 3,286 children, who were attending schools in the city of Aberdeen. Of these children 2,995 took the personality test in 1966; there are complete sets of data for 2,707 children between the ages of 7 and 13 years. The correlational analysis, reported later, is based on the depleted group, whereas the regression analysis is based on the larger group. The following measures have been included in these analyses.

At age 11 years: NFER Non-verbal test 1.

At age 12 years: Moray House Verbal Reasoning test 72.

At age 12 years: Teachers' estimates of English and arithmetic attainment in the primary school, scaled against Moray House attainment tests. This method of scaling imposed on the teachers' average rank-order for each class the mean score and standard deviation obtained by that class in the appropriate standardised test. The final measure averaged attainment in English and arithmetic (see Yates and Pidgeon,[9] p. 88).

At age 13 years: Junior Eysenck Personality Inventory.

At age 13 years: Secondary school teachers' average rank-orders in all academic subjects, scaled on Moray House Advanced Verbal Reasoning test 12.

The intellectual tests were restandardised to a mean of 100 and standard deviation of 15 on the Aberdeen age-group. The internal reliability coefficients of the intellectual tests are all higher than 0·90 and their predictive validities have been repeatedly demonstrated by their use in selection batteries. The JEPI scales have internal reliability coefficients of about 0·80 and test-retest reliability coefficients of about 0·70 at age 13 (Sybil Eysenck[10]). The validity of this instrument has not been clearly demonstrated, except on clinical subjects with extreme symptoms of neuroticism and extraversion.

Results

The analysis in the following section is based on the depleted group of 2,707 children who had complete sets of test scores. In the following analyses "significance" implies a probability level of less than 0·05.

MEANS AND CORRELATION COEFFICIENTS

Table 18.1 shows values similar to those reported by Sybil Eysenck[10] in the JEPI manual. At age 13 years the boys tend to be more extraverted than the girls and also more stable.

TABLE 18.1
Means and Standard Deviations of N, E and L Scores by Sex

| | Boys | | Girls | | Total | |
	Mean	SD	Mean	SD	Mean	SD
Neuroticism	11·832	(4·735)	12·910	(4·432)	12·358	(4·763)
Extraversion	17·858	(3·748)	17·224	(3·620)	17·548	(3·699)
Lie scale	4·154	(2·217)	4·531	(2·359)	4·338	(2·295)
(N)	(1385)		(1322)		(2707)	

The interrelationships between the scores derived from the JEPI (shown in Table 18.2) are also similar to those shown in the manual. The relationship between neuroticism and extraversion is not strictly orthogonal; the values of the correlation coefficients for both boys and

TABLE 18.2

Inter-Correlation Coefficients between the Personality Scales

Scale	Boys		Girls		Total	
	N	E	N	E	N	E
Extraversion	—0·221	—	—0·173	—	—0·206	—
Lie scale	—0·261	—0·068	—0·254	—0·103	—0·246	—0·091

girls are significantly above zero. Although these values are not high, there is still a tendency for the neurotic children to be introverted and for the stable children to be extraverted.

The starting point of this investigation was the question "Is school attainment negatively related to neuroticism and positively related to extraversion?" Tables 18.3 and 18.4 show the values of the correlation coefficients obtained. As the results from the various intellectual tests at different ages show no significant differences, the statistical analysis was limited to the measure of attainment at age 13 years.

The results shown in Table 18.3 support the previous findings. School attainment and neuroticism are negatively related; children with low neuroticism scores tend to occupy higher positions in class than those with high neuroticism scores. The relationship is by no means close, but in this large representative sample it is statistically significant. The relationship is slightly closer for girls than for boys, but this sex difference could have arisen by chance.

TABLE 18.3

Product-moment Correlation Coefficients between Neuroticism and Intellectual Scores at Various Ages by Sex

Test	Age	Boys	Girls	Total
Teachers' Estimates	13	—0·137	—0·185	—0·157
Verbal Reasoning	13	—0·129	—0·158	—0·141
Teachers' Estimates	12	—0·120	—0·163	—0·135
Verbal Reasoning	12	—0·127	—0·143	—0·134
Non-Verbal	11	—0·119	—0·128	—0·123
(N)		(1385)	(1322)	(2707)

Table 18.4 presents a different pattern of relationships. The correlations between extraversion and school attainment are small and could

TABLE 18.4

Product-moment Correlation Coefficients between Extraversion and Intellectual Scores at Various Ages by Sex

Test	Age	Boys	Girls	Total
Teachers' Estimates	13	—0·021	0·064	0·018
Verbal Reasoning	13	0·018	0·084	0·048
Teachers' Estimates	12	—0·001	0·083	0·035
Verbal Reasoning	12	0·022	0·080	0·050
Non-Verbal	11	0·035	0·083	0·058
(N)		(1385)	(1322)	(2707)

have occurred by chance. There is, however, an interesting sign difference between the correlation coefficients obtained for boys and for girls. This sex difference is statistically significant and will be shown by the following regression analysis to be distinct.

REGRESSION ANALYSIS

The next stage was to test the second hypothesis. Are the relationships between the personality dimensions and school attainment non-linear? Previous studies suggested that they might well be non-linear. A regression analysis was applied to data from all 2,995 children who completed the personality inventory, but it was limited to a single attainment measure, namely the teachers' estimates at age 13 years. Mean attainment quotients at five different levels of neuroticism and four different levels of extraversion were calculated, keeping the sexes separate. This allowed the variation of attainment with neuroticism or extraversion to be plotted graphically. Linearity or non-linearity shows up clearly using

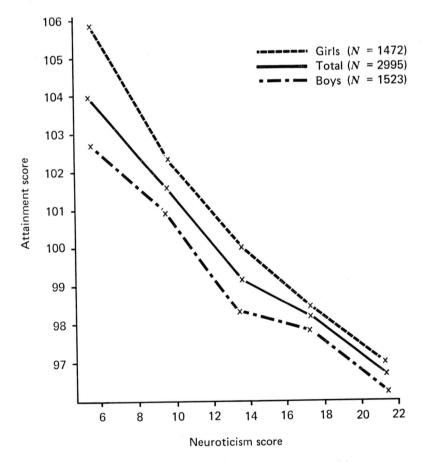

Fig. 18.1 Regression lines for attainment on neuroticism.

this approach. An analysis of variance method (McNemar,[11] pp. 275-81) was used to test whether the relationships were significantly non-linear.

Figure 18.1 suggests that the relationship between neuroticism and attainment is approximately linear. The analysis of variance showed no significant divergence from linearity ($F=0 \cdot 99$ with *df* of 2990 and 3). Again the relationship is similar for boys and girls. The hypothesis of non-linearity and in particular of an inverted-U relationship must be emphatically rejected on this evidence.

The same is not true for extraversion, as can be seen from Fig. 18.2. For the whole group there is a U-shaped relationship and this is significantly non-linear ($F=4 \cdot 32$ with *df* of 2990 and 2). This non-linearity explains the low value of the correlation coefficient reported earlier, correlation being inappropriate for describing a non-linear relationship. The analysis by sexes separately explains the shape of the overall curve. It is a composite curve which combines two quite different relationships. For girls there is a positive relationship between extraversion and attainment, but for boys the relationship is negative.

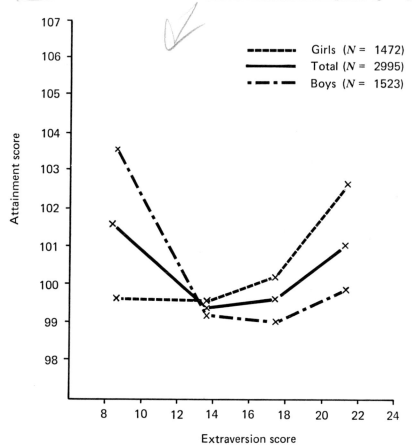

Fig. 18.2 Regression lines for attainment score on extraversion.

Rushton[4] and Hallworth[5] found that extraversion and attainment were positively correlated, whereas Child[6] produced an opposite finding, using a sample which may have included more boys than girls. The sex difference indicated in the above analysis could account for these contradictory findings.

It had become clear by this stage in the investigation that the relationships between the personality dimensions and attainment were far from being simple. To show how attainment varied with extraversion at each level of neuroticism, mean quotients were calculated for nine different personality types for each sex.

Both Table 18.5 and Table 18.6 show that the stable child, whether boy or girl, tends to have a slightly higher position in class than the neurotic child at all levels of extraversion. Table 18.5 shows that the introverted boy tends to be more successful at all levels of neuroticism, but the boys in the "stable introvert" category form a distinctly superior group. Table 18.6 shows a tendency for the extraverted girl to show a higher level of attainment, but this is less strongly marked. Girls who are "stable extraverts" have the highest mean attainment score.

TABLE 18.5

Mean Scores on Secondary School Criterion of BOYS of Differing Personality Types

JEPI Score	High 'E' (24—18)	(N)	Middle 'E' (17—12)	(N)	Low 'E' (11—0)	(N)	All 'E' groups	(N)
High 'N' (24—16)	97·60	(108)	96·80	(73)	102·74	(34)	98·14	(215)
Middle 'N' (15—10)	97·56	(315)	98·14	(206)	97·70	(36)	97·78	(557)
Low 'N' (9—0)	101·14	(516)	101·62	(198)	111·06	(37)	101·76	(751)
All 'N' groups	99·53	(939)	99·38	(477)	103·92	(107)	99·79	(1523)

TABLE 18.6

Mean Scores on Secondary School Criterion of GIRLS of Differing Personality Types

JEPI Score	High 'E' (24—18)	(N)	Middle 'E' (17—12)	(N)	Low 'E' (11—0)	(N)	All 'E' groups	(N)
High 'N' (24—16)	97·28	(110)	98·68	(116)	95·53	(34)	97·68	(260)
Middle 'N' (15—10)	99·99	(325)	98·72	(273)	100·79	(37)	99·49	(635)
Low 'N' (9—0)	104·79	(330)	102·45	(212)	102·57	(35)	103·80	(577)
All 'N' groups	102·67	(765)	100·03	(601)	99·69	(106)	100·86	(1472)

The final stage of this investigation was to test the hypothesis that among the brightest children, the "neurotic introverts" would form the superior group on school attainment. For this analysis the punched cards for all those children with attainment quotients of 110 and above were re-sorted into the same personality categories as before. The mean scores for these contrasting personality types among bright boys and girls are shown in Tables 18.7 and 18.8.

In this final analysis the numbers of children in the cells are, in several instances, too small to allow any significant differences to emerge.

In Table 18.8 the bright girls show exactly the same pattern as the girls in the complete ability range; "stable extraverts" form the superior group on school attainment. Again it appears that "stability" of personality is the most important characteristic as far as school attainment is concern d. The extraversion dimension appears to be less closely related to attainment.

TABLE 18.7

Mean Scores on Secondary School Criterion of BRIGHT BOYS of Differing Personality Types

JEPI Score	High 'E' (24—18)	(N)	Middle 'E' (17—12)	(N)	Low 'E' (11—0)	(N)	All 'E' groups	(N)
High 'N' (24—16)	119·37	(19)	117·10	(11)	118·67	(12)	118·55	(42)
Middle 'N' (15—10)	116·56	(56)	118·19	(42)	119·92	(12)	117·55	(110)
Low 'N' (9—0)	117·87	(144)	118·49	(67)	123·00	(20)	118·50	(231)
All 'N' groups	117·66	(219)	118·25	(120)	120·98	(44)	118·23	(383)

TABLE 18.8

Mean Scores on Secondary School Criterion of BRIGHT GIRLS of Differing Personality Types

JEPI Scores	High 'E' (24—18)	(N)	Middle 'E' (17—12)	(N)	Low 'E' (11—0)	(N)	All 'E' groups	(N)
High 'N' (24—16)	116·53	(21)	118·52	(23)	112·84	(6)	117·00	(50)
Middle 'N' (15—10)	118·11	(72)	118·29	(70)	118·82	(11)	118·24	(153)
Low 'N' (9—0)	119·17	(120)	119·16	(74)	117·67	(15)	119·06	(209)
All 'N' groups	118·55	(213)	118·71	(167)	117·16	(32)	118·50	(412)

Among the bright boys the situation is less clear; the pattern emerging from this analysis is rather different from that obtained with the complete ability range. Among these boys Table 18.7 shows that stability appears to be less important than introversion. Again the small groups involved demand caution in interpretation, but there is at least a suggestion that introversion is more closely related to attainment in this sample than is stability. It is still true, however, that the group with the highest mean attainment score is that of the "stable introverts". There is no suggestion amongst either boys or girls that the "neurotic introverts" are more successful in their schoolwork.

Tests of statistical significance on the "all *E*" and "all *N*" groups in Tables 18.5—18.8 support the above interpretations. In the complete ability range the differences in mean attainment scores for boys both between the neurotic and stable extreme groups and between the extravert and introvert extreme groups are significant. In the results for bright boys, however, only the difference between extravert and introvert is significant. Among the girls in the complete ability range, the difference in mean attainment scores between the neurotic and stable extreme groups is significant, but there is no significant difference on the extraversion dimension. This result was also found with the bright girls.

Conclusions and Discussion

A sample of over 2,700 children provides results which can be treated with more confidence than those from many of the previous studies with samples which were small and often unrepresentative. The initial four hypotheses oversimplified the pattern of relationships which emerged from this investigation. Simple verification or rejection of each separate hypothesis was impossible, as the following summary of results shows.

(1) Neuroticism shows a significant correlation with school attainment. Children with high neuroticism scores tend to be less successful than those with low neuroticism scores. This is true for both boys and girls. The relationship is not curvilinear and thus the correlation coefficient ($-0 \cdot 16$) gives a true indication of the degree of relationship.

(2) Extraversion shows no significant correlation with school attainment, because a distinct sex difference produces an overall non-linear relationship. Extraverted girls and introverted boys tend to be more successful in school work than children with the opposite personality characteristics.

(3) Girls who are "stable extraverts" and boys who are "stable introverts" show the highest mean attainment scores. This is also true of the brightest children. The hypothesis that "neurotic introverts" would be the most superior group among bright children must be rejected.

Each of these findings clarifies particular points arising from previous studies. The essential linearity of the relationship between neuroticism and school attainment is contrary to Lynn and Gordon's[3] findings. They extended the use of the Yerkes-Dodson law to human subjects to predict a non-linear relationship. However, the Yerkes-Dodson law is adaptable; for simple tasks high drive (which Eysenck links with neuroticism) facilitates learning; for tasks of moderate complexity an inverted-U relationship is predicted; while for difficult tasks high drive interferes with learning efficiency. As we do not know which tasks in human learning can be equated with those which are difficult for rodents, no firm predictions can be made from the law. Brown[12] has suggested that even in animal learning experiments, there is insufficient evidence to substantiate it. The extension into human learning is thus highly speculative. Those who wish to use Eysenck's theoretical framework relating neuroticism to drive level and also the Yerkes-Dodson law relating "drive level" to task performance will find support from the present findings. But they will have to assume that the teacher confronts his class with "difficult tasks". The children at least would support this view.

It has already been suggested that the sex difference on the extraversion dimension may explain previous contradictory findings. But why extraversion should be an advantage for girls in their schoolwork, but a disadvantage for boys, is not at all clear. It may be that girls act out their extraversion, especially stable extraversion, in a more scholastically acceptable way than do the boys. Perhaps the values of the boys' peer groups tend to be in opposition to academic success. Presumably extraverted boys will participate in these groups more actively than the introverts and this might result in a less successful academic record. If the values supported by the girls' peer groups supported academic success, this might account for the sex difference which has been identified.

The superiority of the introverted boy is not difficult to explain in terms of the behaviour patterns ascribed to the introvert by Eysenck[13] (p. 59): "The typical introvert . . . is a quiet retiring sort of person, introspective, fond of books rather than people; he is reserved and distant except with intimate friends. He tends to plan ahead, 'looks before he leaps', and distrusts the impulse of the moment. . . . He keeps his feeling under close control, seldom behaves in an aggressive manner, and does not lose his temper easily. He is reliable, somewhat pessimistic, and places great value on ethical standards."

In terms of Eysenck's theoretical formulation of personality structure, the introvert should also be at an advantage in school learning. Eysenck suggests that the extravert builds up reactive inhibition more quickly than the introvert. This interferes with the learning process and prevents the extravert from being able to concentrate on the learning task for more than short periods of time. Thus, from both behaviour patterns and Eysenck's personality theory, the introvert should reach a higher standard, on average, than the extravert in school work. But why should this be true of boys and not of girls? Does the female introvert withdraw too completely from normal class interaction in the learning process and thus fail to learn as effectively as the introverted boy?

Finally, the hypothesis that, among bright children, "neurotic introversion" would be associated with scholastic success had to be rejected. The relationships found among the university students cannot be simply a result of selecting the brightest school children. Perhaps, as intelligent children grow older, they also become more self-critical and their scores on self-report inventories move towards the neurotic end of the scales. Or perhaps the self-reliance expected at university level actually makes students who take their responsibilities seriously become neurotic.

This study has perhaps thrown some new light on the problem of personality relationships with school attainment, but the impression it must leave is of complex interrelationships about which we still know all too little.

References

[1] W. D. FURNEAUX, "The Psychologist and the University", *University Quarterly*, 1962, **17**, pp. 33-47.

[2] R. KELVIN, C. LUCAS and A. OJHA, "The Relationship between Personality, Mental Health and Academic Performance in University Students", *British Journal of Social and Clinical Psychology*, 1965, **4**, pp. 244-53.

[3] R. LYNN and I. GORDON, "The Relationship of Neuroticism and Extraversion to Intelligence and Educational Attainment", *British Journal of Educational Psychology*, 1961, **31**, pp. 194-203.

[4] J. RUSHTON, "The Relationship between Personality Characteristics and Scholastic Success in 11-year-old Children", *British Journal of Educational Psychology*, 1966, **36**, pp. 178-84.

[5] H. J. HALLWORTH, "Personality Ratings of Adolescents: A Study in a Comprehensive School", *British Journal of Educational Psychology*, 1964, **34**, pp. 171-77.

[6] D. CHILD, "The Relationships between Introversion-Extraversion, Neuroticism and Performance in School Examinations", *British Journal of Educational Psychology*, 1964, **34**, pp. 187-95.

[7] H. J. EYSENCK and P. O. WHITE, "Personality and the Measurement of Intelligence", *British Journal of Educational Psychology*, 1964, **34**, pp. 197-201.

[8] J. D. NISBET and N. J. ENTWISTLE, *The Age of Transfer to Secondary Education*, University of London Press, London, 1966.

[9] A. YATES and D. A. PIDGEON, *Admission to Grammar Schools*, Newnes, London, 1957.

[10] S. B. G. Eysenck, *J.E.P.I. Manual*, University of London Press, London, 1965.

[11] Q. McNEMAR, *Psychological Statistics*, John Wiley & Sons, New York, 1962.

[12] W. P. BROWN, "The Yerkes-Dodson Law Repealed", *Psychological Reports*, 1965, **17**, pp. 663-66.

[13] H. J. EYSENCK, *Fact and Fiction in Psychology,* Penguin Books, London, 1965.

ACKNOWLEDGEMENTS

The "Age of Transfer" project is sponsored by the Scottish Council for Research in Education. We are grateful for the cooperation of the Directors of Education from both Aberdeen town and county. In particular we should like to acknowledge the help of all the many teachers who administered the tests and supplied class orders of merit.

Chapter 19

A Follow-up Study of School Achievement in Relation to Personality

D. S. FINLAYSON
School of Education, University of Liverpool

The relationships between extraversion, neuroticism and the school achievements of a group of 128 boys at the ages of 12, 13 and 14 in a grammar school were examined using the method of "zone analysis". In the 11+ tests, no systematic differences between the groups were noted, but once in the secondary school, introverts obtained progressively higher marks in yearly examinations than extraverts. In introverts, low neuroticism is consistently associated with better achievement, while in extraverts high neuroticism steadily depresses academic performance over the three years to give significant overall effect in the third year. If the achievements of only the two high neurotic groups are considered, introverts tend to improve with age while extraverts deteriorate.

Introduction

The two personality dimensions of extraversion and neuroticism have been studied in relation to educational achievement by a number of workers, and Rushton,[1] after a review of the literature indicating the conflicting nature of their findings, suggests that age might be an important variable in interpreting results. Warburton (personal communication, 1969) has grouped studies using Cattell's 16 PF or Eysenck's personality measures according to whether they involve primary school children, children from 11-15, adolescents from 15-18, or adults of more than 18 years of age. He regards 15 as a crucial age, and of neuroticism effects he states: "Up to the age of 15, anxiety is never an advantage, but at later ages, it is so in 24 out of 34 cases." Of introversion he states: "Before the age of 15 the introversion factors

From the *British Journal of Educational Psychology*, 1970, **40**, pp. 344-49. Reprinted by permission of D. S. Finlayson and the *British Journal of Educational Psychology*.

are an advantage in only 13 per cent of the cases, but after 15, the figure rises to 96 per cent."

Most of the studies which have investigated relationships between personality dimensions and academic achievement have employed correlation techniques. Eysenck[2] has criticised such methods on two counts. Firstly, linearity of regression cannot be assumed if the Yerkes-Dodson law is held to apply to neuroticism effects; and secondly, such methods do not allow any investigation to be made of interaction effects between the dimensions. He suggests that a more appropriate method to use is "zone analysis". For this, with personality variables, subjects would be placed in groups according to their scores on both the major dimensions. Furneaux[3] has used this method of "zone analysis" with university students, and Child[4] with secondary school children. This latter study, however, included children of different ages and used only a very crude measure of academic achievement.

In this paper, the method of "zone analysis" is used to study the relationships between extraversion and neuroticism with school achievement in groups of boys in a grammar school. Their achievements are examined when they are 12, 13 and 14 and hence any changes in the pattern of relationships as the children approach the crucial age of 15 can thus be noted.

Design

The boys were given the Junior Eysenck Personality Inventory at the beginning of their second year in the school. A median split was made in the distribution of scores on each of the personality scales, thus securing four groups—for both introverts and extraverts, there were groups with high and low neuroticism scores. After excluding boys who had left the schools within the three years or who had been absent from the yearly examinations held during that time, the number of boys within each of the personality groups was equalised by random selection so that a two-by-two analysis of variance design could be applied to the data. Each of the four groups comprised 32 boys.

The 11+ verbal reasoning scores of the four personality groups were first examined. From the non-significant F ratios, it was concluded that any differences in achievement which were demonstrated between the

TABLE 19.1

Mean Extraversion, Neuroticism and Verbal Reasoning Scores of Personality Groups

Degree of neuroticism	Test	Extraverts	Introverts
Low	Extraversion	21·34	16·13
	Neuroticism	7·00	7·50
	VRQ	126·00	126·44
		N = 32	N = 32
High	Extraversion	21·44	16·00
	Neuroticism	14·91	16·31
	VRQ	125·22	124·50
		N = 32	N = 32

groups could not be attributed to this factor. The mean scores of the four groups in the personality scales and verbal reasoning test are given in Table 19.1.

Two measures of school achievement were used: (i) the AQ and EQ scores obtained in the 11+ examination; (ii) the scores in four internal academic subject examinations—English, mathematics, science and a foreign language—held at the end of each of the first three years. One common paper was given to all classes and scripts were marked in most subjects by the same markers throughout. Where this was not done, the marks were scaled, using the combined 11+ quotient total as the common measure. The marks were then standardised and the total score taken as the second measure of school achievement.

The hypotheses tested were:

1. there are no differences between extravert and introvert groups in school achievement;
2. there are no differences between high and low neuroticism groups in school achievement;
3. the interaction of extraversion/introversion and neuroticism has no effect on school achievement.

Results

The scores of each of the personality groups in each of the two 11+ objective tests and in the school examinations are shown in Table 19.2, and the *F* ratios of the effects in Table 19.3.

TABLE 19.2

Mean Scores of Personality Groups

Degree of neuroticism	EQ		AQ		1st Year Examination		2nd Year Examination		3rd Year Examination	
	Extra.	Intro.	Extra.	Intro.	Extra.	Intro.	Extra.	Intro.	Extra.	Intro.
Low	118·81	121·84	124·09	124·94	187·50	223·59	194·37	232·62	190·50	235·87
High	121·28	120·00	123·16	122·50	191·22	195·82	180·72	206·09	171·78	210·84

TABLE 19.3

F **Ratios of Personality Effects on Achievement**

Effect	EQ	AQ	1st Year	2nd Year	3rd Year
Extraversion	< 1	< 1	3·213	9·702 **	14·666 **
Neuroticism	< 1	1·705	1·124	3·871	3·929 *
Interaction	2·845	< 1	1·926	< 1	< 1

* $p < 0.05$.
** $p < 0.01$.

In neither of the 11+ tests are there any systematic differences in the group scores. Once in the secondary school, however, in all three years, introverts of both levels of neuroticism achieved better than their corresponding extravert groups. The size of the differences between these groups was not significant in the first year, but became increasingly significant in the second and third years. Hypothesis 1 can thus be rejected with increasing confidence.

Neuroticism effects are rather more complex. Looking at introverts and extraverts separately, low neuroticism is consistently associated with better achievement in introverts, but with extraverts high neuroticism steadily depresses academic performance over the three years to a degree which produces a significant overall effect in the third year.

If the relative performance of the two high neurotic groups are examined over the five achievement measures, it will be seen that at the age of 11 it is the extraverted group who are marginally better than their introverted equivalents in both the selection tests. In the first year of the secondary school, the difference has now swung marginally in favour of the introverted group. In the second and third years, this tendency for the neurotic introverts to improve with age, and for the neurotic extraverts to deteriorate, steadily increases. It was not possible to test the significance of such contrary trends in the form of an interaction effect as the year groups were correlated, but the significance of the changes in secondary school performance in each of the high neurotic groups was tested separately, and the F ratios are shown in Table 19.4. The significant F ratios for individuals merely indicate that the scores in the three examinations were correlated. In the case of extraverts the changes over time were large enough to reach significance, and with introverts their magnitude, though well marked, fell short of significance. There seems little doubt, therefore, that the contrary direction of these changes over time are not due to chance factors.

TABLE 19.4

F **Ratios of High Neurotic Groups Over Three Examinations**

		Between years	Amongst individuals
	Extraverts	3·241 *	9·841 * *
High neurotics			
	Introverts	2·659	14·203 * *

* $p < 0.05$.
** $p < 0.01$.

Discussion

In these results, there is supportive evidence for the view that the effects of both introversion and neuroticism on the academic achievement of boys increase with age. In this sample, introversion showed a significant relationship with achievement when the boys were between 12 and 13 in the second year. The degree of confidence in the relationship was increased in the following year when they were 13/14. With neuroticism the relationship with achievement also became closer as the boys became older and reached the significance level when they were 13/14. These ages are slightly earlier than the crucial age of 15 suggested by Warburton, but it is important to bear in mind the highly selected nature of the sample. Of high ability, these boys were in a school where academic expectations were extremely high and where a boy's motivation and ability to sustain application and concentration for protracted periods would be of considerable importance. It may be that these effects are not so much a consequence of chronological age itself, as of increasing pressures and expectations from the educational system. Further studies with girls, with pupils of lower ability levels, and in schools where academic expectations are less demanding, are clearly required.

The contrary effect of neuroticism, according to whether the subjects are introverts or extraverts, is of considerable interest both theoretically and methodologically. From a theoretical point of view, some explanation is required why high neuroticism should have contrary effects on extraverts and introverts. Methodologically, this finding amply justifies Eysenck's view that correlational methods have serious limitations when applied to personality data and that interactional effects between the dimensions themselves warrant a place in research designs.

References

[1] J. RUSHTON, "The Relationship between Personality Characteristics and Scholastic Success in 11-Year-Old Children", *British Journal of Educational Psychology*, 1966, **36**, pp. 178-84.

[2] H. J. EYSENCK, "Personality and Experimental Psychology", *Bulletin of the British Psychological Society*, 1966, **19**, pp. 1-28.

[3] W. D. FURNEAUX, "The Psychologist and the University", *University Quarterly*, 1962, **17**, pp. 33-47.

[4] D. CHILD, "The Relationships between Introversion/Extraversion, Neuroticism and Performance in School Examinations", *British Journal of Educational Psychology*, 1964, **34**, pp. 187-96.

ACKNOWLEDGEMENT

The data for this study were collected as part of a larger project financed by the Department of Education and Science.

Subject Index

Author Index